Table of Contents

[Interior Title Page](#)

[Copyright Page](#)

[Dedication Page](#)

[About the Author](#)

[Forward](#)

[Section 1: Butterflies and Native Plants](#)

[Section 2: Resources to Help ID Native Plants](#)

[Section 3: Butterfly Garden Requirements](#)

[Section 4: Adult Butterfly Food](#)

[Section 5: Butterfly Host Plants](#)

[Section 6: Butterfly Moisture Requirements](#)

[Section 7: Butterfly Shelter Requirements](#)

[Section 8: Butterfly Predation](#)

[Section 9: Central Florida Butterflies and Their Native Host Plants](#)

[Section 10: Swallowtail Butterflies and Their Host Plants](#)

[Section 11: White Butterflies and Their Host Plants](#)

[Section 12: Sulphur Butterflies and Their Host Plants](#)

[Section 13: Blue Butterflies and Their Host Plants](#)

[Section 14: Hairstreak Butterflies and Their Host Plants](#)

[Section 15: Hackberry Butterflies and Their Host Plants](#)

[Section 16: Milkweed Butterflies and Their Host Plants](#)

[Section 17: Longwing Butterflies and Their Host Plants](#)

[Section 18: Brushfooted Butterflies and Their Host Plants](#)

[Section 19: Metalmark Butterfly and Its Host Plants](#)

[Section 20: Nymphs and Satyr Butterflies and Their Host Plants](#)

Section 21: Spread Winged Skipper Butterflies and Their Host Plants

Section 22: Duskywing Skipper Butterflies and Their Host Plants

Section 23: Branded Skipper Butterflies and Their Host Plants

Section 24: Giant Skipper Butterflies and Their Host Plants

Section 25: Native Nector Sources: Wildflowers

Section 26: Native Nector Sources: Trees

Section 27: Native Nector Sources: Shrubs

Section 28: Native Nector Sources: Vines

Bibliography

Index

Central Florida Butterflies
And Their Host Plants

A Complete List of Native Host Plants

by Sharon R. LaPlante

2018

This work is the intellectual property of Sharon R. LaPlante and may not be produced, stored or transmitted in any form, or by any means, including mechanical or electronic without the prior permission from the author. You know what happens if you steal my stuff … a thousand deer ticks will invade your private parts.

For more information about Central Florida's native plants and wildlife visit Sharons Florida (http://sharonsflorida.com).

To buy native seeds stop by one of my stores:

Sharon's Florida Shopify Store (https://sharons-florida-store.myshopify.com/)

Sharon's Florida Ebay store (https://www.ebay.com/str/sharonsflorida)

Copyright of Sharon's Florida. Copyright © 2018 Sharon R. LaPlante

Dedicated to all the people who love and nurture pollinators.

About the Author

Sharon was born and raised in Tampa, Florida and for over 40 years has studied, gardened, landscaped, and enjoyed Florida's plant and animal ecosystems. Sharon noticed a long time ago that the Florida normally depicted in movies and magazines is not 'authentic Florida', but is rather a glitzy, often gaudy, cosmopolitan Miami-kind of Florida, which is quite different from most of the rest of the Sunshine State. The Florida Sharon loves is a delightfully diverse collection of local plant and wildlife habitats from hardwood hammocks, with their several hundred year old oaks, to saw grass marshes and inland waterways with their manatees and otters. Once you move inland from Florida's coastal beaches, you soon discover a world of surprising diversity and beauty. A place where the fox or the bobcat is as likely to appear as is the palm tree in the tourism poster. It is these lesser known habitats about which Sharon lives, studies, and writes.

Sharon's first passion was wildlife rehabilitation, however, this evolved into the study of native plants, and Florida plant communities; the fundamental systems that provide food and shelter for her beloved Florida fauna.

Several years ago Sharon founded the Hernando Chapter of the Florida Native Plant Society in an effort to bring together people who had an interest in the native plants of central Florida, particularly Hernando County. Sharon greatly enjoyed acting as the conduit between academia, institutional and governmental interests, and the grass roots, community interests regarding plant and animal ecosystems.

Sharon discovered that serving others with a common interest in endemic plants and animals to be deeply rewarding, and the plant society the perfect outlet for this endeavor. During this period, Sharon was also a Master Gardener with the Hernando County Extension Office, and would later be offered a position by Hernando County to run its just-created, 'Florida Yards & Neighborhoods' program. Unfortunately, a life-changing illness prevented Sharon from accepting this position.

Sharon has had several articles published in Eco-Florida magazine and many of her botanical photographs were used in Gil Nelson's book, Florida's Best Native Landscape Plants, and the Florida Association of Florida Native Plant Nurseries Guide. Sharon also created and developed her own website, SharonsFlorida, (http://www.sharonsflorida.com) where hundreds of visitors from all over the globe visit monthly to view articles and photos of local plants and wildlife.

Sharon in her garden

Forward

My goal for this book was to create a reference that contained a complete list of butterfly host plants that are native to central Florida.

I prefer landscaping with native plants, however, there is not much information out there that is easily accessible and reliable, so, I have assembled my own collection of information into a quick reference guide accessible to everyone.

The main sections of the book focus on listing the butterflies that can be found in central Florida and the host plants they use for larval foods.

At the end of the book are tables which consolidate data about flowering native plants that provide nectar for butterflies. The information included shows common names, botanical names, flower color, flower bloom period, size, light, and moisture requirements. My selection is based on experience with butterflies using the blooms of the native trees, shrubs, wildflowers, and vines that are provided in each table.

If you have ever wanted to try butterfly gardening in our area you will find this work to be very helpful in choosing native plants to achieve success. My guide will help the central Florida gardener decide what native plants to choose that support each variety of butterfly, at each of their life-stages. Actually, the basic principles I discuss in the book can be applied to creating a butterfly garden wherever on Earth it may be.

I am confident that with a little effort, and perseverance, both the novice and experienced butterfly gardener will discover in these pages a sure pathway to a bountiful butterfly landscape. Of course, butterfly gardening has a learning curve and experience is always king so go forth and garden!

Thank you for purchasing my book.

**You are on your way to creating
a great butterfly garden!**

A zebra longwing butterfly (*Heliconius charithonia*) nectaring on a giant ironweed (*Vernonia gigantea*) flower.

Section 1

Butterflies and Native Plants

A zebra longwing caterpillar (*Heliconius charithonia*) eating a corkystem passionvine leaf (*Passiflora suberosa*).

Backyard butterfly gardening is a rewarding endeavor as well as a valuable contribution everyone can make to the health of the environment and the native butterfly population.

Attracting butterflies to your yard, or garden, is easier than you may think because the plants that are an integral part of a butterfly's life cycle grow unattended all around us. With minimal effort these natives can be incorporated into our private gardens.

Florida's native butterflies use Florida native plants, it's that simple. There really is no trick to it. The butterflies that pass through your landscape are native to our region of Florida and as such have evolved to use our native plants to survive. Your ability to identify these native plants will enhance your butterfly gardening experience ten-fold. By taking advantage of natives, the plants that evolved to thrive in the native habitats, the butterfly gardener saves time, money, labor, and gives the butterflies what they need.

Take advantage of the wonderful native plants that Florida has to offer and you automatically provide for many of our beautiful native butterflies. Native wildflowers such as Spanish needles and lyre leaf sage are invaluable nectar sources for feeding adult butterflies and can be found growing in lawns, garden beds, parking lots, and roadsides. Florida milkpea and toadflax, two examples of natives considered "useless weeds", provide larval food for butterflies without any work on the part of the gardener as they readily volunteer wherever allowed.

Give a little space and some time to these natives in your garden and let them flower. Let them reseed. This will be a win for both butterfly and you. My humble garden becomes absolutely crowded at times with these fascinating and beautiful creatures. With minimal planning and care, your efforts will be handsomely rewarded.

Section 2

Resources to Help ID Native Plants

A gray hairstreak butterfly (*Strymon Melinus*) laying eggs on an eastern milkpea vine (*Galactia volubilis*).

By simply making room in the home landscape for the native plants and wildflowers they require, the gardener is rewarded with an abundance of delightful butterflies and caterpillars to study, photograph, or just enjoy watching. The key to taking advantage of free native butterfly plants, is first being able to identify them. Once you learn what they are you can then selectively allow them to thrive in your garden. You might be surprised by how soon the butterflies and their young begin to appear.

There are many great resources for learning native plant identification. Of course nothing beats hands-on field study. So get a field guide, or an app, and head out into natural areas to familiarize yourself with the native plants and wildflowers around you.

A very helpful app called Florida Wildflowers (Play Store, iStore) was developed by the creator of Wildflowersearch.org, and includes over 2,500 species of plants found in Florida. Searching for specific plants can be done by a variety of search criteria such as color, habitat, leaf shape, etc.

The Atlas of Florida Plants (http://www.florida.plantatlas.usf.edu/) has a wonderful collection of native plant photographs and is a great choice for internet searches, but you will need to know the specific name(s) of the plants you are looking for.

The Lady Bird Johnson Wildflower Center (https://www.wildflower.org/plants/) has an amazing native plant database with tons of information and can be searched by scientific name, common name or plant family.

Craig Huegel is located in Central Florida and has many years of experience with native plants so please be sure to visit his site, Hawthorn Hill Wildflowers, (http://hawthornhillwildflowers.blogspot.com/) to glean his first hand experience with natives or buy one of his great books on Amazon like Native Wildflowers and Other Ground Covers for Florida Landscapes

For Florida plant identification field guides, both Walter Kingsley Taylor's and Gil Nelson's books are great choices. Walter Kingsley Taylor's The Guide to Florida Wildflowers is the perfect choice for the beginner because it is organized by the color of the wildflower and very easy to navigate. Gil Nelson's books, The Trees of Florida and The Shrubs and Woody Vines of Florida, will provide you with help in identifying Florida trees, shrubs and woody vines.

Of course, sometimes we want instant gratification and purchasing native plants is an option. However, main-stream retail outlets always seem to make this process difficult because their native plant selection is limited or non-existent. So I would suggest you visit the Florida Association of Native Nurseries (https://www.afnn.org/) web site to locate a native plant nursery near you.

Whirlabout skipper *(Polites vibex)* resting on Spanish needles *(Bidens alba)*

Section 3

Butterfly Garden Requirements

The giant swallowtail butterfly's (*Papilio cresphontes*) life cycle from a caterpillar, to a chrysalis, to an adult [left to right].

A butterfly requires two entirely different types of plants in order to complete its life cycle. Flying adult butterflies drink flower nectar and their crawling offspring chew on plant parts. What this means, essentially, is that the butterfly gardener should provide both nectaring flowers for the adults, and foliage for the caterpillars. The food required for both larval (catepillar) and adult life stages should be planted, or cultivated, in order to develop a successful and abundant butterfly garden. The more butterfly plants you grow ... the more butterflies you will have hanging around your garden.

An adult butterfly is equipped with a proboscis, or tubular tongue, that it uses for drawing in liquid. Immature butterflies, known as larvae or caterpillars, have chewing mouth parts and feed on the leaves and stems of their host plants.

Additional requirements for a successful butterfly garden include water and shelter. However, these are usually met without additional effort once the butterfly garden becomes established and filled with plants.

An often overlooked subject is the use of chemicals in the butterfly garden. This is the absolute worst possible idea. You cannot control Mother Nature, but you can decide not to kill your butterflies outright. These delicate creatures have enough working against them. Pesticides are antithetical to the goal of creating a natural habitat in which butterflies can thrive. Poisons mean indiscriminate death ... do not use them in your butterfly garden ... ever. Don't even use insecticidal soap ... butterflies and caterpillars are insects and soap will kill them.

Section 4

Adult Butterfly Food

A white peacock butterfly (*Anartia jatrophae*) resting on sweetgum tree (*Liquidambar styraciflua*) leaves.

Adult butterflies fly and drink nectar from flowers. However, there are some species such as the tawny emperor, and the mourning cloak, that also take advantage of tree sap and even carrion.

Planting an abundance of flowering trees, shrubs, vines and wildflowers, will provide lots of food choices for the adult butterflies. If you compost your fruit scraps leave them exposed, on the top of your compost pile, because many butterflies will take advantage of the sugary fruit in addition to your flowers.

Fortunately, native plants come in all shapes and sizes and grow in a variety of conditions. Each native plant grows in a particular Florida habitat, or plant community, and being aware of this helps the gardener place the plant in its preferred growing environment. Of course, modern landscaping is not the same as a native habitat, however, paying attention to the light and moisture levels of a particular area will dictate what will grow there without fighting mother nature. The ultimate goal would be to recreate a natural habitat structure with layers of vegetation from the tallest tree to the lowest ground cover. Locating the plant in the right place will ensure full potential growth and flowering of your natives and the success of your butterfly garden.

Balance and variety should be the goal. Luckily, neither butterfly nor nature require a neat and tidy landscape. Every square inch of a butterfly garden can be planted with one thing or another. Gardening with Native Plants of the South is a great basic primer to use as a guide to layering your landscape with natives. I would recommend any new butterfly gardner consider adding this to his or her library.

When planting nectar plants keep in mind that adult butterflies need sunlight in order to warm their wings for flight. So, although it is important to have flowers growing in full sun it is not imperative to have only sun loving plants. Butterflies will fly into sunny spots early in the day to warm their wings and then head off to all parts of the garden to forage for nectar until sunset. Balance and variety will ensure a range of different butterflies because all have their own sun and shade location preferences. Some butterflies prefer hot sunny areas of the garden while others take refuge in shady spots. You will begin to notice sun and shade preferences at the species level as well as for individual butterflies. If you plant it ... they will come - and provide a fascinating variety of species for enjoyment and study.

Zebra longwings, and other black butterflies, prefer shady areas much more frequently than do their lighter cousins. Their dark color readily absorbs heat thus enabling them to be active sooner in the day as well as on cooler days. Loitering in the sun too long causes them to overheat so they tend to gather around the more shady areas of the landscape.

Fill all the nooks and crannies with native plants and the butterflies will take advantage of your thoughtfulness. The end result will be greater numbers of individuals and species coming to visit your butterfly garden.

Section 5

Butterfly Host Plants

A pipevine swallowtail butterfly (*Battus philenor*) laying eggs on a woolly Dutchman's pipevine (*Aristolochia tomentosa*) plant.

Baby butterflies, also known as catepillars, eat plant leaves and tender new growth until they are sufficiently mature to form a chrysalis and metamorphize into an adult, flying butterfly.

Each butterfly variety uses a particular plant family to support their offspring. Adult female butterflies must lay their eggs on specific plants, called host plants, so that when the young hatch they have the right food, the food with which they evolved, to eat.

Growing an abundance, as well as a variety, of host plants will attract and support the largest possible population of butterfly babies to your garden. The female butterfly searches for the proper host plant on which to lay her eggs by tasting each plant with sensors on her feet. Once located, she will lay her eggs on its tips where the tender new growth is found. Caterpillars prefer to feed on tender new growth, but when that becomes scarce they will eat the outer covering of the plant stalks, stems, and immature seed pods.

Planting one individual host plant will most likely attract a female butterfly to deposit her eggs, but it will soon be defoliated and will fail to provide enough food to satisfy the hungry, growing caterpillars. Therefore, planting host plants in a variety of locations throughout your landscape will ensure that a particular plant will not be eaten as quickly and will have time to bounce back faster with new growth. Also, if a host plant is eaten down to nothing, additional plants in alternate locations ensures there will be other areas in your garden where hungry caterpillars can be moved to if need be. Of course, this depends upon the size of the plant and the size of your available space. You certainly don't need more than one black cherry tree, but four or five separate plantings of swamp milkweeds are doable even in a small space and provide quite a lot of monarch caterpillar food. Some plants will still be decimated and some caterpillars may still go hungry. Striving for harmony can be a little stressful for the new butterfly gardener. However, be patient and you will soon see that a balance between butterfly caterpillars and host plants, with occasional exceptions, will be achieved.

It is all well and good that butterfly gardeners rush to the store to purchase dill and parsley for their black swallowtail caterpillars, but butterflies really need natural plants in order for them to have a sustainable population. The hundreds of other butterfly species that aren't lucky enough to have easy to purchase larval food go hungry and their numbers decrease. A balanced butterfly garden should allow, and provide, for common species that aren't showy and popular like long tailed skippers, or Phaon crescent.

Caterpillars feed continuously for a few weeks during which time they grow considerably. Each time the caterpillar gets too large for its skin it completes a molt, which is when it sheds its old skin for a new, larger one. During these periods, it stops eating and moves to an-out-of-the-way spot on the plant, most often at the base near the ground, and is very still for a day or so until the molt is complete. Each molt stage, or instar, as it is called, furthers the caterpillar's development and they typically experience four or five instars before entering their last developmental stage called pupation. The baby will soon become a flying butterfly!

Pupation is when the larval structures break down and adult structures such as wings, proboscis, and antennae, are formed. To prepare for this metamorphosis the caterpillar will move several feet away from the host plant and attach itself to a nearby shrub or structure. Some species will descend into the leaf litter to begin this stage. During pupation, the caterpillar will shed its skin for the last time, but instead of another skin, will develop a very hard outer covering called a chrysalis. Metamorphosis takes place inside this crysalis. After about two weeks an adult butterfly will emerge and trigger a repeat of this fascinating life cycle.

Section 6

Butterfly Moisture Requirements

A cloudless sulphur butterfly (*Phoebis sennae*) obtaining moisture and nutrients from a bird dropping after a recent rain.

A butterfly drinks by uncoiling its proboscis (tubular tongue) and inserting it in the crevices of the mulch or along the edge of a water droplet drawing water through its tube-shaped tongue. The smallest amount of moisture, or droplet of water, can provide a good drink for a thirsty butterfly.

A butterfly's moisture requirements are usually met in the form of raindrops, water droplets, moist soils, moistened mulches, and animal droppings. Routine watering of the butterfly garden is generally more than adequate to fulfill their moisture needs. Watering the flowerbeds on hot days will usually result in several butterflies landing to drink from the moist soil or mulch.

As unlikely as it sounds, butterflies are also attracted to misting, or spraying, water. I use a bird mister regularly to water my landscape because it puts out a fine mist rather than a heavy spray, and within minutes of turning it on butterflies show up along with the many songbirds.

Butterflies can often be seen drinking, or puddling, from mud puddles and areas of concentrated livestock urine in order to obtain required salts and minerals as well as water. They also procure moisture, and minerals, from fresh manure such as bird droppings, horse, and cow manure. Butterflies certainly know where to find needed nutrients.

Section 7

Butterfly Shelter Requirements

A zebra swallowtail butterfly (*Eurytides marcellus*) resting in the undergrowth during inclement weather.

Adult butterflies use mature foliage for protection from inclement weather, predators, or merely to rest. Therefore, shelter requirements are generally met once the butterfly garden begins to become established with foliage. Trees and shrubs provide large areas that allow butterflies to rest in between, and underneath, the leaves.

Brightly painted butterfly houses are very attractive in the garden, but unfortunately, at least for this author, do not seem to entice butterflies into the confined space they provide and are mainly for aesthetics.

Butterflies are wary creatures for the most part and need a quick means of escape, so they prefer to roost in areas that are easy to fly in and out of like the branches of trees and shrubs. The areas in between the foliage gives them adequate cover and an easy escape route if threatened by predators. In my garden the undersides of firebush and beautyberry leaves seem to be favorite roosting spots. The large leaves of these two species also provide the butterflies a place of refuge during our frequent summer rain showers.

Some species of butterfly, such as the zebra longwing, roost communally in the long, draping, clumps of Spanish moss. Several dozen may be found resting with closed wings, close by each other and their food source, but the entire group will explode into movement if disturbed.

Section 8

Butterfly Predation

A red spotted purple butterfly (*Limenitis arthemis*) resting on a black cherry tree (*Prunus serotina*) leaf.

The sad truth is that most of your butterflies, both immature and adult, will be preyed upon. Butterflies are low on the food chain and are consumed by lots of other species of wildlife. Unfortunately, where there is food, there will often be predators appearing to take advantage of it. Predation is a harsh and distressing aspect of butterfly gardening, but this is nature's way, and as such, we must deal with it. Natural predation should perhaps be viewed as a good thing because it generally shows that a balance has been achieved and a food chain has been established. A butterfly garden with an overabundance of caterpillars is not natural. Generally there isn't going to be enough food to get the caterpillars through all instars to pupation. After all, Mother Nature designed butterflies and catepillars to provide food for other creatures.

Butterflies are an important part of this natural food chain. Were it not for butterflies many other animals would go hungry and be unable to complete their life cycles. Putting a positive mental spin on it helps to alleviate the stress of seeing these creatures, which you have coaxed and nurtured, being preyed upon. It is frustrating, but learning and understanding their vital role in nature's bigger picture will help to ease this frustration.

Butterflies, and caterpillars, provide food for a great many creatures. Butterfly eggs are eaten by insects such as lady bugs and their larvae, and some are even eaten by other caterpillars as they consume plant leaves. Caterpillars are parasitized by ichneumon wasps, and eaten by predators such as ants, toads, birds, wasps, and lizards. Adult butterflies are eaten by birds, preying mantis, and many other creatures looking for a meal.

Toads do not generally go out of their way to hunt catepillars, but they are opportunistic feeders and will eat a caterpillar when they encounter one. Wasps and songirds, on the other hand, will hunt endlessly for caterpillars in order to feed their young. Springtime usually brings on a flush of emerging caterpillars just in time for hungry baby birds. Paper wasps will carry off caterpillars to insert into their nests to feed their young. Ichneumon wasps lay their eggs on the caterpillars themselves to provide a living food area for their young. The poor caterpillars are being used for food sources left and right, but it is the natural progression of things.

Dealing with predators, or not, is of course up to the butterfly gardener. I tend to leave things alone and let them follow a natural course. The best way to deal with predators is to manually remove them with either hot water or clear tape. For certain species, like assassin bugs, if they get too out of control, I catch them off guard and knock them into a cup of hot, soapy, water. End of assassin bugs! If aphids really creep you out remove them with sticky tape. Wrap a piece of tape inside out around a finger tip and press it gently against the aphids so they stick to it ... being careful not to harm the plant ... then toss them. Spraying chemicals, whether poison or simple dish soap, is harmful to butterflies and is not acceptable in a butterfly garden. After all, providing a safe habitat for butterflies is the goal ... not killing them.

Section 9

Central Florida Butterflies and Their Native Host Plants

A monarch butterfly caterpillar (*Danaus plexippus*) eating a sandhill milkweed seed pod (*Asclepias humistrata*).

Each of the following sections provides the name, and plant family, of the native plants that each buterly uses as a host plant. Common names are often misleading, and vary from geographical locations, so the botanical name is listed as well. The common and scientific name for each particular butterfly is also given.

If you plant it ... they will come, but be sure to plant enough.

Section 10: Swallowtail Butterflies and Their Host Plants
Section 11: White Butterflies and Their Host Plants
Section 12: Sulphur Butterflies and Their Host Plants
Section 13: Blue Butterflies and Their Host Plants
Section 14: Hairstreak Butterflies and Their Host Plants
Section 15: Hackberry Butterflies and Their Host Plants
Section 16: Milkweed Butterflies and Their Host Plants
Section 17: Longwing Butterflies and Their Host Plants
Section 18: Brushfooted Butterflies and Their Host Plants
Section 19: Metalmark Butterfly and Its Host Plants
Section 20: Nymphs and Satyr Butterflies and Their Host Plants
Section 21: Spread Winged Skipper Butterflies and Their Host Plants
Section 22: Duskywing Skipper Butterflies and Their Host Plants
Section 23: Branded Skipper Butterflies and Their Host Plants
Section 24: Giant Skipper Butterflies and Their Host Plants

Section 10

Swallowtail Butterflies and Their Host Plants

Black Swallowtail (*Papilio polyxenes*)

Apiaceae
(celery family)

Chaerophyllum tainturieri (hairyfruit chervil)
Cicuta maculata (spotted water hemlock)
Cryptotaenia canadensis (Canadian honewort)
Daucus pusillus (American wild carrot)
Eryngium aquaticum (rattlesnakemaster)
Eryngium aromaticum (fragrant eryngo)
Eryngium baldwinii (Baldwin's eryngo)
Eryngium prostratum (creeping eryngo)
Eryngium yuccifolium (button rattlesnakemaster)
Lilaeopsis carolinensis (Carolina grasswort)
Lilaeopsis chinensis (eastern grasswort)
Ptilimnium capillaceum (mock Bishop's weed)
Sanicula canadensis (Canadian blacksnakeroot)
Spermolepis divaricata (roughfruit scaleseed)
Spermolepis echinata (bristly scaleseed)
Tiedemannia filiformis (water cowbane)
Trepocarpus aethusae (white nymph)
Zizia aurea (golden alexanders)
Zizia trifoliate (meadow alexanders)

Giant Swallowtail (*Papilio cresphontes*)

Rutaceae
(citrus family)

Amyris elemifera (sea torchwood)
Ptelea trifoliate (hoptree)
Zanthoxylum americanum (prickly ash)
Zanthoxylum clava-herculis (Hercule's club)
Zanthoxylum fagara (lime prickly ash)

Palamedes Swallowtail (*Papilio palamedes*)

Lauraceae
(laurel family)

Cassytha filiformis (love vine)
Lindera benzoin (spicebush)
Litsea aestivalis (pondspice)
Ocotea coriacea (lancewood)
Persea borbonia var. borbonia (red bay)
Persea borbonia var. *humilis* (silk bay)
Persea palustris (swamp bay)
Sassafras albidum (sassafras)

Pipevine Swallowtail (*Battus philenor*)

Aristolochiaceae
(birthwort family)

Aristolochia serpentaria (Virginia snakeroot)
Aristolochia tomentosa (woolly dutchman's pipe)

Polydamas Swallowtail (*Battus polydamas*)

Aristolochiaceae
(birthwort family)

Aristolochia serpentaria (Virginia snakeroot)
Aristolochia tomentosa (woolly dutchman's pipe)

Spicebush Swallowtail (*Papilio troilus*)

Lauraceae
(laurel family)

Cassytha filiformis (love vine)
Lindera benzoin (spicebush)
Litsea aestivalis (pondspice)
Ocotea coriacea (lancewood)
Persea borbonia var. *borbonia* (red bay)
Persea borbonia var. *humilis* (silk bay)
Persea palustris (swamp bay)
Sassafras albidum (sassafras)

Tiger Swallowtail (*Papilio glaucus*)

Magnoliaceae
(magnolia family)

Liriodendron tulipifera (tulip tree)
Magnolia grandiflora (southern magnolia)
Magnolia virginiana (sweetbay)

Zebra Swallowtail (*Eurytides marcellus*)

Annonaceae
(custard apple family)

Annona glabra (pond apple)
Asimina angustifolia (slimleaf pawpaw)
Asimina incana (woolly pawpaw)
Asimina manasota (Manasota pawpaw)
Asimina obovata (bigflower pawpaw)
Asimina parviflora (smallflower pawpaw)
Asimina pulchella (pretty false pawpaw)
Asimina pygmea (dwarf pawpaw)
Asimina reticulata (netted pawpaw)

Section 11

White Butterflies and Their Host Plants

Cabbage White (*Pieris rapae*)

Brassicaeae
(mustard family)

Cakile edentula (American searocket)
Cynophalla flexuosa (bayleaf capertree)
Cardamine bulbosa (spring cress)
Quadrella jamaicensis (Jamaican capertree)

Checkered White (*Pontia protodice*)

Brassicaeae
(mustard family)
Cakile edentula (American searocket)
Cynophalla flexuosa (bayleaf capertree)
Cardamine bulbosa (spring cress)
Quadrella jamaicensis (Jamaican capertree)

Great Southern White (*Ascia monuste*)

Brassicaeae
(mustard family)

Cakile edentula (American searocket)
Cynophalla flexuosa (bayleaf capertree)
Cardamine bulbosa (spring cress)
Quadrella jamaicensis (Jamaican capertree)

Section 12

Sulphur Butterflies and Their Host Plants

Barred Yellow (*Eurema daira*)

Fabaceae

(pea family)

Aeschynomene americana (shyleaf)
Aeschynomene pratensis (meadow joint vetch)
Aeschynomene viscidula (sticky joint vetch)
Stylosanthes biflora (sidebeak pencilflower)
Stylosanthes hamata (cheesytoes)

Cloudless Sulphur (*Phoebis sennae*)

Fabaceae

(pea family)

Senna ligustrina (privet wild sensitive plant)
Senna marilandica (Maryland wild sensitive plant)
Senna obtusifolia (sicklepod)

Dainty Sulphur (*Nathalis iole*)

Asteraceae

(aster family)

Bidens alba (beggarticks)
Bidens bipinnata (Spanish needles)
Bidens laevis (smooth beggarticks)
Bidens mitis (small fruit beggarticks)

Large Orange Sulphur (*Phoebis agarithe*)

Fabaceae

(pea family)

Lysiloma latisiliquum (false tamarind)
Pithecellobium unguis-cati (cat claw blackbead)

Little Yellow (*Pyrisitia lisa*)

Fabaceae

(pea family)

Chamaecrista fasciculata (partridge pea)
Chamaecrista nictitans (sensitive pea)

Orange Barred Sulphur (*Phoebis philea*)

Fabaceae

(pea family)

Senna ligustrina (privet wild sensitive plant)
Senna marilandica (Maryland wild sensitive plant)
Senna obtusifolia (sicklepod)

Orange Sulphur (*Colias eurytheme*)

Fabaceae
(pea family)

Trifolium carolinianum (Carolina clover)
Trifolium reflexum (buffalo clover)

Sleepy Orange (*Abaeis nicippe*)

Fabaceae
(pea family)

Senna ligustrina (privet wild sensitive plant)
Senna marilandica (Maryland wild sensitive plant)
Senna obtusifolia (sicklepod)

Southern Dogface (*Zerene cesonia*)

Fabaceae
(pea family)

Amorpha fruticosa (bastard false indigo)
Amorpha herbacea var. *herbacea* (clusterspike false indigo)
Dalea adenopoda (summer farewell)
Dalea carnea var. *albida* (white tassels)
Dalea carnea var. *carnea* (white tassels)
Dalea feayi (Feay's prarie clover)
Dalea pinnata (summer farewell)

Pearl Crescent *(Phyciodes tharos)* nectoring on sandhill milkweed *(Asclepias humistriata)*

Section 13

Blue Butterflies and Their Host Plants

Cassius Blue (*Leptotes cassius*)

Plumbaginaceae
(plumbago family)

Plumbago zeylanica (doctorbush)

Ceraunus Blue (*Hemiargus ceraunus*)

Fabaceae
(pea family)

Centrosema arenicola (pineland butterfly pea)
Centrosema virginianum (spurred butterfly pea)
Galactia elliottii (Elliott's milkpea)
Galactia floridana (Florida milkpea)
Galactia mollis (soft milkpea)
Galactia purshii (Pursh's milkpea)
Galactia volubilis (Eastern milkpea)
Vigna luteola (hairypod cowpea)

Eastern Pygmy Blue (*Brephidium pseudofea*)

Amaranthaceae

(amaranth family)

Salicornia ambigua (perennial glasswort)
Salicornia bigelovii (annual glasswort)

Section 14

Hairstreak Butterflies and Their Host Plants

Banded Hairstreak (*Satyrium calanus*)

Juglandaceae
(hickory family)

Carya aquatica (water hickory)
Carya floridana (scrub hickory)
Carya glabra (pignut hickory)
Carya tomentosa (mockernut hickory)

Fagaceae
(oak family)

Quercus chapmanii (Chapman's oak)
Quercus geminata (sand live oak)
Quercus incana (bluejack oak)
Quercus inopina (scrub oak)
Quercus laevis (turkey oak)
Quercus laurifolia (laurel oak)
Quercus margarettae (sand post oak)
Quercus michauxii (swamp chestnut oak)
Quercus minima (dwarf live oak)
Quercus myrtifolia (myrtle oak)

Quercus nigra (water oak)
Quercus pumila (running oak)
Quercus virginiana (live oak)

Gray Hairstreak (*Strymon melinus*)

Fabaceae
(pea family)

Desmodium canescens (hoary ticktrefoil)
Desmodium ciliare (hairy small-leaf ticktrefoil)
Desmodium floridanum (Florida ticktrefoil)
Desmodium glabellum (Dillenius' ticktrefoil)
Desmodium paniculatum (panicled ticktrefoil)
Desmodium perplexum (perplexed ticktrefoil)
Desmodium strictum (pinebarren ticktrefoil)
Desmodium tenuifolium (slimleaf ticktrefoil)
Desmodium viridiflorum (velvetleaf ticktrefoil)
Galactia elliottii (Elliott's milkpea)
Galactia floridana (Florida milkpea)
Galactia mollis (soft milkpea)
Galactia purshii (Pursh's milkpea)
Galactia volubilis (Eastern milkpea)

Malvaceae
(mallow family)

Kosteletzkya pentacarpos (Virginia saltmarsh mallow)

Great Purple Hairstreak (*Atlides halesus*)

Viscaceae
(mistletoe family)

Phoradendron leucarpum (oak mistletoe)

Red-banded Hairstreak (*Calycopis cecrops*)

Myricaceae
(bayberry family)

Morella caroliniensis (Northern bayberry)
Morella cerifera (wax myrtle)

Anacardiaceae
(sumac family)

Rhus copallinum (winged sumac)

Southern Hairstreak (*Satyrium favonius*)

Fagaceae
(oak family)

Quercus chapmanii (Chapman's oak)
Quercus geminata (sand live oak)
Quercus Incana (bluejack oak)
Quercus inopina (scrub oak)
Quercus laevis (turkey oak)
Quercus laurifolia (laurel oak)
Quercus margarettae (sand post oak)
Quercus michauxii (swamp chestnut oak)
Quercus minima (dwarf live oak)
Quercus myrtifolia (myrtle oak)
Quercus nigra (water oak)
Quercus pumila (running oak)
Quercus virginiana (live oak)

Striped Hairstreak (*Satyrium liparops*)

Rosaceae
(rose family)

Crataegus aestivalis (may haw)
Crataegus crus-galli (cockspur hawthorn)
Crataegus marshallii (parsley hawthorn)
Crataegus michauxii (Michaux's hawthorn)
Crataegus uniflora (dwarf hawthorn)
Crataegus viridis (green hawthorn)

Ericaceae
(heath family)

Vaccinium arboreum (sparkleberry)

White - M Hairstreak (*Parrhasius m album*)

Fagaceae
(oak family)

Quercus chapmanii (Chapman's oak)
Quercus geminata (sand live oak)
Quercus incana (bluejack oak)
Quercus inopina (scrub oak)
Quercus laevis (turkey oak)
Quercus laurifolia (laurel oak)
Quercus margarettae (sand post oak)
Quercus michauxii (swamp chestnut oak)
Quercus minima (dwarf live oak)
Quercus myrtifolia (myrtle oak)
Quercus nigra (water oak)
Quercus pumila (running oak)
Quercus virginiana (live oak)

Section 15

Hackberry Butterflies and Their Host Plants

American Snout (*Libytheana carinenta*)

Celtis
(hackberry family)

Celtis iguanaea (iguana hackberry)
Celtis laevigata (hackberry)

Hackberry Butterfly (*Asterocampa celtis*)

Celtis
(hackberry family)

Celtis iguanaea (iguana hackberry)
Celtis laevigata (hackberry)

Tawny Emperor (*Asterocampa clyton*)

Celtis
(hackberry family)

Celtis iguanaea (iguana hackberry)
Celtis laevigata (hackberry)

Cloudless sulphur catepillar *(Phoebis sennae)* feeding on non-native valamuerto (*Senna pendula* var. *glabrata)*

Section 16

Milkweed Butterflies and Their Host Plants

Monarch (*Danaus plexippus*)

Apocynaceae
(dogbane family)

Asclepias amplexicaulis (clasping milkweed)
Asclepias cinerea (Carolina milkweed)
Asclepias connivens (large flower milkweed)
Asclepias curtissii (Curtiss' milkweed)
Asclepias feayi (Florida milkweed)
Asclepias humistrata (pinewoods milkweed)
Asclepias incarnata (swamp milkweed)
Asclepias lanceolata (few-flower milkweed)
Asclepias longifolia (long-leaf milkweed)
Asclepias pedicellata (savannah milkweed)
Asclepias perennis (swamp milkweed)
Asclepias tomentosa (velvet-leaf milkweed)
Asclepias tuberosa (butterfly milkweed)
Asclepias verticillata (whorled milkweed)
Asclepias viridis (green antelope-horn)
Asclepias viridula (green milkweed)
Cynanchum northropiae (fragrant swallow-wort)
Funastrum clausum (white twine-vine)
Matelea floridana (Florida milkvine)
Matelea pubiflora (trailing milkvine)
Orthosia scoparia (leafless swallow-wort)

Queen (*Danaus gilippus*)

Apocynaceae
(dogbane family)

Asclepias amplexicaulis (clasping milkweed)
Asclepias cinerea (Carolina milkweed)
Asclepias connivens (large flower milkweed)
Asclepias curtissii (Curtiss' milkweed)
Asclepias feayi (Florida milkweed)
Asclepias humistrata (pinewoods milkweed)
Asclepias incarnata (swamp milkweed)
Asclepias lanceolata (few-flower milkweed)
Asclepias longifolia (long-leaf milkweed)
Asclepias pedicellata (savannah milkweed)
Asclepias perennis (swamp milkweed)
Asclepias tomentosa (velvet-leaf milkweed)
Asclepias tuberosa (butterfly milkweed)
Asclepias verticillata (whorled milkweed)
Asclepias viridis (green antelope-horn)
Asclepias viridula (green milkweed)
Cynanchum northropiae (fragrant swallow-wort)
Funastrum clausum (white twine-vine)
Matelea floridana (Florida milkvine)
Matelea pubiflora (trailing milkvine)
Orthosia scoparia (leafless swallow-wort)

Soldier (*Danaus eresimus*)

Apocynaceae
(dogbane family)

Asclepias amplexicaulis (clasping milkweed)
Asclepias cinerea (Carolina milkweed)
Asclepias connivens (large flower milkweed)

Asclepias curtissii (Curtiss' milkweed)
Asclepias feayi (Florida milkweed)
Asclepias humistrata (pinewoods milkweed)
Asclepias incarnata (swamp milkweed)
Asclepias lanceolata (few-flower milkweed)
Asclepias longifolia (long-leaf milkweed)
Asclepias pedicellata (savannah milkweed)
Asclepias perennis (swamp milkweed)
Asclepias tomentosa (velvet-leaf milkweed)
Asclepias tuberosa (butterfly milkweed)
Asclepias verticillata (whorled milkweed)
Asclepias viridis (green antelope-horn)
Asclepias viridula (green milkweed)
Cynanchum northropiae (fragrant swallow-wort)
Funastrum clausum (white twine-vine)
Matelea floridana (Florida milkvine)
Matelea pubiflora (trailing milkvine)
Orthosia scoparia (leafless swallow-wort)

Section 17

Longwing Butterflies and Their Host Plants

Gulf Fritillary (*Agraulis vanilla*)

Passifloraceae
(passionvine family)

Passiflora incarnata (purple passionflower)
Passiflora lutea (yellow passionflower)
Passiflora suberosa (corkystem passionflower)

Variegated Fritillary (*Euptoieta claudia*)

Passifloraceae
(passionvine family)

Passiflora incarnata (purple passionflower)
Passiflora lutea (yellow passionflower)
Passiflora suberosa (corkystem passionflower)

Violaceae
(violet family)

Viola bicolor (field pansy)
Viola lanceolata (bog white violet)
Viola palmata (early blue violet)
Viola primulifolia (primrose leaf violet)
Viola sororia (common blue violet)
Viola villosa (Carolina violet)

Viola walteri (prostrate blue violet)

Zebra Longwing (*Heliconius charithonia*)

Passifloraceae
(passionvine family)

Passiflora lutea (yellow passionflower)
Passiflora suberosa (corkystem passionflower)

Section 18

Brushfooted Butterflies and Their Host Plants

American Lady (*Vanessa virginiensis*)

Asteraceae

(aster family)

Artemisia campestris subsp. *caudata* (field wormwood)
Gamochaeta antillana (delicate everlasting)
Gamochaeta argyrinea (silvery cudweed)
Gamochaeta purpurea (spoonleaf cudweed)
Vernonia angustifolia (tall ironweed)
Vernonia blodgettii (Florida ironweed)
Vernonia gigantea (giant ironweed)

Buckeye (*Junonia coenia*)

Orobanchaceae

(broom-rape family)

Agalinis divaricata (pineland false foxglove)
Agalinis fasciculata (beach false foxglove)
Agalinis filicaulis (Jackson false foxglove)
Agalinis filifolia (Seminole false foxglove)
Agalinis harperi (Harper's false foxglove)
Agalinis laxa (twoline false foxglove)
Agalinis linifolia (flaxleaf false foxglove)

Agalinis maritima (saltmarsh false foxglove)
Agalinis obtusifolia (tenlobe false foxglove)
Agalinis plukenetii (Plukenet's false foxglove)
Agalinis purpurea (purple false foxglove)
Agalinis setacea (threadleaf false foxglove)
Agalinis tenuifolia (slenderleaf false foxglove)
Buchnera americana (American bluehearts)
Linaria canadensis (Canada toadflax)
Linaria floridana (Apalachicola toadflax)
Seymeria cassioides (yaupon blacksenna)
Seymeria pectinate (piedmont blacksenna)

Florida Leafwing (*Anaea troglodyte floridalis*)

Euphorbiaceae
(spurge family)

Croton argyranthemus (silver croton)
Croton capitatus (woolly croton)
Croton glandulosus (vente conmigo)
Croton michauxii (Michaux's croton)
Croton punctatus (beach croton)

Painted Lady (*Vanessa cardui*)

Asteraceae
(aster family)

Cirsium horridulum (purple thistle)
Cirsium nuttallii (Nuttall's thistle)

Pearl Crescent (*Phyciodes tharos*)

Asteraceae
(aster family)

Symphyotrichum adnatum (scale-leaf aster)
Symphyotrichum bahamense (Bahama aster)
Symphyotrichum carolinianum (climbing aster)
Symphyotrichum concolor (Eastern silver aster)
Symphyotrichum dumosum (rice button aster)
Symphyotrichum elliottii (Elliott's aster)
Symphyotrichum lateriflorum (Florida water aster)
Symphyotrichum pilosum (white oldfield aster)
Symphyotrichum simmondsii (Simmond's aster)
Symphyotrichum tenuifolium (perennial saltmarsh aster)
Symphyotrichum undulatum (wavy leaf aster)
Symphyotrichum walteri (Walter's aster)

Phaon Crescent (*Phyciodes phaon*)

Verbenaceae
(vervain family)

Phyla nodiflora (turkey tangle fogfruit)

Question Mark (*Polygonia interrogationis*)

Celtis
(hackberry family)

Celtis iguanaea (iguana hackberry)
Celtis laevigata (hackberry)

Ulmaceae
(elm family)

Ulmus alata (winged elm)
Ulmus americana (American elm)
Ulmus crassifolia (cedar elm)

Urticaceae
(nettle family)

Urtica chamaedryoides (heartleaf nettle)
Urtica urens (dwarf nettle)

Red Admiral (*Vanessa atalanta*)

Urticaceae
(nettle family)

Boehmeria cylindrica (false nettle)
Parietaria floridana (Florida pellitory)
Parietaria praetermissa (clustered pellitory)
Urtica chamaedryoides (heartleaf nettle)
Urtica urens (dwarf nettle)

Red Spotted Purple (*Limenitis arthemis*)

Malvaceae
(mallow family)

Tilia americana var. *caroliniana* (Carolina basswood)

Rosaceae
(rose family)

Prunus americana (American plum)
Prunus angustifolia (chickasaw plum)
Prunus caroliniana (cherry laurel)
Prunus geniculata (scrub plum)
Prunus serotina (black cherry)
Prunus umbellata (flatwoods plum)

Salicaceae

(willow family)

Populus alba (white poplar)
Populus deltoides (Eastern cottonwood)
Salix caroliniana (coastal plain willow)
Salix floridana (Florida willow)

Seminole Texan Crescent (*Anthanassa texana*)

Acanthaceae

(acanthus family)

Justicia angusta (pineland waterwillow)
Justicia ovata var. *ovata* (loose flower waterwillow)
Justicia pringlei (Cooley's water willow)

Viceroy (*Limenitis archippus*)

Populus

(poplar family)

Populus alba (white poplar)
Populus deltoids (Eastern cottonwood)

Salicaceae

(willow family)

Salix caroliniana (coastal plain willow)
Salix floridana (Florida willow)

White Peacock (*Anartia jatrophae*)

Plantaginaceae
(plantain family)

Bacopa caroliniana (lemon bacopa)
Bacopa innominata (tropical water hyssop)
Bacopa monnieri (herb-of-grace)

Verbenaceae
(vervain family)

Phyla nodiflora (turkey tangle fogfruit)

Section 19

Metalmark Butterfly and Its Host Plants

Little Metalmark (*Calephelis virginiensis*)

Asteraceae
(aster family)

Cirsium horridulum (purple thistle)
Cirsium muticum (swamp thistle)
Cirsium nuttallii (Nuttall's thistle)

Section 20

Nymphs and Satyr Butterflies and Their Host Plants

Appalachian Brown (*Satyrodes appalachia*)

Cyperaceae
(sedge family)

Carex alata (broadwing sedge)
Carex atlantica subsp. *capillacea* (prickly bog sedge)
Carex basiantha (Willdenow's sedge)
Carex blanda (eastern woodland sedge)
Carex bromoides (brome-like sedge)
Carex chapmannii (Chapman's sedge)
Carex cherokeensis (Cherokee sedge)
Carex comosa (long-hair sedge)
Carex complanata (blue sedge)
Carex crebriflora (coastal plain sedge)
Carex crus-corvi (raven-foot sedge)
Carex dasycarpa (sandy woods sedge)
Carex debilis (white-edge sedge)
Carex digitalis (slender woodland sedge)
Carex elliottii (Elliott's sedge)
Carex fissa var. *aristata* (hammock sedge)
Carex frankii (Frank's sedge)
Carex gholsonii (Gholson's sedge)
Carex gigantean (giant sedge)
Carex glaucescens (clustered sedge)
Carex hyalinolepis (shoreline sedge)
Carex intumescens (greater bladder sedge)
Carex joorii (cypress swamp sedge)
Carex leptalea (bristly-stalked sedge)
Carex longii (Long's sedge)

Carex lupuliformis (false hop sedge)
Carex lurida (shallow sedge)
Carex nigromarginata var. *floridana* (blackedge sedge)
Carex oxylepis (sharp-scale sedge)
Carex paeninsulae (peninsula sedge)
Carex retroflexa (reflexed sedge)
Carex stipata (awl-fruit sedge)
Carex striata (Walter's sedge)
Carex styloflexa (bent sedge)
Carex tribuloides (blunt broom sedge)
Carex verrucosa (warty sedge)
Carex vexans (Florida hammock sedge)

Carolina Satyr (*Hermeuptychia sosybius*)

Poaceae
(grass family)

Chasmanthium laxum (slender wood-oats)
Chasmanthium nitidum (shiny wood-oats)
Chasmanthium sessiliflorum (longleaf wood-oats)
Paspalum bifidum (pitch fork crown-grass)
Paspalum boscianum (bull crown-grass)
Paspalum botterii (rustyseed paspalum)
Paspalum caespitosum (blue crown-grass)
Paspalum conjugatum (sour paspalum)
Paspalum dissectum (mudbank crowngrass)
Paspalum distichum (knotgrass)
Paspalum eglume (Florida reimargrass)
Paspalum floridanum (Florida paspalum)
Paspalum leave (field paspalum)
Paspalum plicatulum (brown seed paspalum)
Paspalum praecox (early paspalum)
Paspalum pubiflorum (hairy seed paspalum)
Paspalum repens (water paspalum)
Paspalum setaceum (thin paspalum)
Paspalum vaginatum (seashore paspalum)
Urochloa adspersa (Dominican signal-grass)
Urochloa platyphylla (broadleaf signal-grass)

Common Wood Nymph (*Cercyonis pegala*)

Poaceae

(grass family)

Tridens ambiguous (pine barren fluff grass)
Tridens carolinianus (Carolina fluff grass)
Tridens flavus (purpletop fluff-grass)

Gemmed Satyr (*Cyllopsis gemma*)

Poaceae

(grass family)

Chasmanthium laxum (slender wood-oats)
Chasmanthium nitidum (shiny wood-oats)
Chasmanthium sessiliflorum (longleaf wood-oats)

Georgia Satyr (*Neonympha areolatus*)

Poaceae

(grass family)

Sorghastrum elliottii (slender indian-grass)
Sorghastrum nutans (yellow indian-grass)
Sorghastrum secundum (lopsided indian-grass)

Southern Pearly Eye (*Enodia portlandia*)

Poaceae
(grass family)

Arundinaria gigantea (switchcane)

Viola's Wood Satyr (*Megisto viola*)

Poaceae
(grass family)

Stenotaphrum secundatum (St. Augustine grass)

Section 21

Spread Winged Skipper Butterflies and Their Host Plants

Confused Cloudywing (*Thorybes confuses*)

Fabaceae
(pea family)

Desmodium canescens (hoary ticktrefoil)
Desmodium ciliare (hairy small-leaf ticktrefoil)
Desmodium floridanum (Florida ticktrefoil)
Desmodium glabellum (Dillenius' ticktrefoil)
Desmodium paniculatum (panicled ticktrefoil)
Desmodium perplexum (perplexed ticktrefoil)
Desmodium strictum (pinebarren ticktrefoil)
Desmodium tenuifolium (slimleaf ticktrefoil)
Desmodium viridiflorum (velvetleaf ticktrefoil)

Dorantes Longtail (*Urbanus dorantes*)

Fabaceae
(pea family)

Desmodium canescens (hoary ticktrefoil)
Desmodium ciliare (hairy small-leaf ticktrefoil)
Desmodium floridanum (Florida ticktrefoil)
Desmodium glabellum (Dillenius' ticktrefoil)
Desmodium paniculatum (panicled ticktrefoil)

Desmodium perplexum (perplexed ticktrefoil)
Desmodium strictum (pinebarren ticktrefoil)
Desmodium tenuifolium (slimleaf ticktrefoil)
Desmodium viridiflorum (velvetleaf ticktrefoil)

Hayhurst's Scallopwing (*Staphylus hayhurstii*)

Amaranthaceae
(amaranth family)

Iresine diffusa (Juba's bush)

Long-tailed Skipper (*Urbanus proteus*)

Fabaceae
(pea family)

Centrosema arenicola (pineland butterfly pea)
Centrosema virginianum (spurred butterfly pea)
Clitoria fragrans (sweet scented pigeon-wings)
Clitoria mariana (Atlantic pigeon-wings)
Desmodium canescens (hoary ticktrefoil)
Desmodium ciliare (hairy small-leaf ticktrefoil)
Desmodium floridanum (Florida ticktrefoil)
Desmodium glabellum (Dillenius' ticktrefoil)
Desmodium paniculatum (panicled ticktrefoil)
Desmodium perplexum (perplexed ticktrefoil)
Desmodium strictum (pinebarren ticktrefoil)
Desmodium tenuifolium (slimleaf ticktrefoil)
Desmodium viridiflorum (velvetleaf ticktrefoil)

Mangrove Skipper (*Phocides pigmalion*)

Rhizophoraceae
(mangrove family)

Rhizophora mangle (red mangrove)

Northern Cloudywing (*Thorybes pylades*)

Fabaceae
(pea family)

Desmodium canescens (hoary ticktrefoil)
Desmodium ciliare (hairy small-leaf ticktrefoil)
Desmodium floridanum (Florida ticktrefoil)
Desmodium glabellum (Dillenius' ticktrefoil)
Desmodium paniculatum (panicled ticktrefoil)
Desmodium perplexum (perplexed ticktrefoil)
Desmodium strictum (pinebarren ticktrefoil)
Desmodium tenuifolium (slimleaf ticktrefoil)
Desmodium viridiflorum (velvetleaf ticktrefoil)

Silver-spotted Skipper (*Epargyreus clarus*)

Fabaceae
(pea family)

Amorpha fruticosa (false indigo)
Amorpha herbacea var. *herbacea* (clusterspike false indigo)

Southern Cloudywing (*Thorybes bathyllus*)

Fabaceae

(pea family)

Desmodium canescens (hoary ticktrefoil)
Desmodium ciliare (hairy small-leaf ticktrefoil)
Desmodium floridanum (Florida ticktrefoil)
Desmodium glabellum (Dillenius' ticktrefoil)
Desmodium paniculatum (panicled ticktrefoil)
Desmodium perplexum (perplexed ticktrefoil)
Desmodium strictum (pinebarren ticktrefoil)
Desmodium tenuifolium (slimleaf ticktrefoil)
Desmodium viridiflorum (velvetleaf ticktrefoil)

Section 22

Duskywing Skipper Butterflies and Their Host Plants

Checkered Skipper (*Pyrgus communis*)

Malvaceae
(mallow family)

Sida ciliaris (bracted fan-petals)
Sida elliottii (Elliott's fan-petals)
Sida rhombifolia (Indian hemp)
Sida ulmifolia (common fan-petals)

Horace's Duskywing (*Erynnis horatius*)

Fagaceae
(oak family)

Quercus chapmanii (Chapman's oak)
Quercus geminata (sand live oak)
Quercus incana (bluejack oak)
Quercus inopina (scrub oak)
Quercus laevis (turkey oak)
Quercus laurifolia (laurel oak)
Quercus margarettae (sand post oak)
Quercus michauxii (swamp chestnut oak)
Quercus minima (dwarf live oak)
Quercus myrtifolia (myrtle oak)
Quercus nigra (water oak)
Quercus pumila (running oak)

Quercus virginiana (live oak)

Juvenal's Duskywing (*Erynnis juvenalis*)

Fagaceae
(oak family)

Quercus chapmanii (Chapman's oak)
Quercus geminata (sand live oak)
Quercus incana (bluejack oak)
Quercus inopina (scrub oak)
Quercus laevis (turkey oak)
Quercus laurifolia (laurel oak)
Quercus margarettae (sand post oak)
Quercus michauxii (swamp chestnut oak)
Quercus minima (dwarf live oak)
Quercus myrtifolia (myrtle oak)
Quercus nigra (water oak)
Quercus pumila (running oak)
Quercus virginiana (live oak)

Sleepy Duskywing (*Erynnis brizo*)

Fagaceae
(oak family)

Quercus chapmanii (Chapman's oak)
Quercus geminata (sand live oak)
Quercus incana (bluejack oak)
Quercus inopina (scrub oak)
Quercus laevis (turkey oak)
Quercus laurifolia (laurel oak)
Quercus margarettae (sand post oak)
Quercus michauxii (swamp chestnut oak)
Quercus minima (dwarf live oak)

Quercus myrtifolia (myrtle oak)
Quercus nigra (water oak)
Quercus pumila (running oak)
Quercus virginiana (live oak)

Tropical Checkered Skipper (*Pyrgus oileus*)

Malvaceae
(mallow family)

Sida ciliaris (bracted fan-petals)
Sida elliottii (Elliott's fan-petals)
Sida rhombifolia (Indian hemp)
Sida ulmifolia (common fan-petals)

Zarucco Duskywing (*Erynnis zarucco*)

Fagaceae
(oak family)

Quercus chapmanii (Chapman's oak)
Quercus geminata (sand live oak)
Quercus incana (bluejack oak)
Quercus inopina (scrub oak)
Quercus laevis (turkey oak)
Quercus laurifolia (laurel oak)
Quercus margarettae (sand post oak)
Quercus michauxii (swamp chestnut oak)
Quercus minima (dwarf live oak)
Quercus myrtifolia (myrtle oak)
Quercus nigra (water oak)
Quercus pumila (running oak)
Quercus virginiana (live oak)

Section 23

Branded Skipper Butterflies and Their Host Plants

Aaron's Skipper (*Poanes aaroni*)

Poaceae
(grass family)

Panicum amarum (bitter panicum)
Panicum dichotomiflorum var. *bartowense* (fall panicgrass)
Panicum hemitomom (maidencane)
Panicum virgatum (switchgrass)

Arogos Skipper (*Atrytone arogos*)

Poaceae
(grass family)

Sorghastrum elliottii (slender indian-grass)
Sorghastrum nutans (yellow indian-grass)
Sorghastrum secundum (lopsided indian-grass)

Baracoa Skipper (*Polites baracoa*)

Poaceae

(grass family)

grasses
(no specific species documented)

Byssus Skipper (*Problema byssus*)

Poaceae

(grass family)

Saccharum alopecuroides (silver plumegrass)
Saccharum baldwinii (narrow plumegrass)
Saccharum giganteum (sugarcane plumegrass)
Tripsacum dactyloides (Eastern gamagrass)

Canna Skipper (*Calpodes ethlius*)

Cannaceae

(canna family)

Canna flaccida (bandanna of the everglades)

Marantaceae

(arrow root family)

Thalia geniculata (alligator flag)

Clouded Skipper (*Lerema accius*)

Poaceae

(grass family)

Panicum amarum (bitter panicum)
Panicum dichotomiflorum var. *bartowense* (fall panicgrass)
Panicum hemitomom (maidencane)
Panicum virgatum (switchgrass)
Saccharum alopecuroides (silver plumegrass)
Saccharum baldwinii (narrow plumegrass)
Saccharum giganteum (sugarcane plumegrass)

Delaware Skipper (*Anatrytone logan*)

Poaceae

(grass family)

Panicum amarum (bitter panicum)
Panicum dichotomiflorum var. *bartowense* (fall panicgrass)
Panicum hemitomom (maidencane)
Panicum virgatum (switchgrass)

Dotted Skipper (*Hesperia attalus*)

Poaceae

(grass family)

Digitaria ciliaris (southern crabgrass)
Digitaria cognata (Carolina crabgrass)
Digitaria filiformis var. *filiformis* (slender crabgrass)
Digitaria floridana (Florida crabgrass)
Digitaria gracillima (longleaf crabgrass)
Digitaria horizontalis (Jamaican crabgrass)
Digitaria insularis (sourgrass)
Digitaria serotina (dwarf crabgrass)
Digitaria simpsonii (Simpson's crabgrass)
Panicum amarum (bitter panicum)

Panicum dichotomiflorum var. *bartowense* (fall panicgrass)
Panicum hemitomom (maidencane)
Panicum virgatum (switchgrass)

Dun Skipper (*Euphyes vestris*)

Cyperaceae
(sedge family)

Carex alata (broadwing sedge)
Carex atlantica subsp. *capillacea* (prickly bog sedge)
Carex basiantha (Willdenow's sedge)
Carex blanda (eastern woodland sedge)
Carex bromoides (brome-like sedge)
Carex chapmannii (Chapman's sedge)
Carex cherokeensis (Cherokee sedge)
Carex comosa (long-hair sedge)
Carex complanata (blue sedge)
Carex crebriflora (coastal plain sedge)
Carex crus-corvi (raven-foot sedge)
Carex dasycarpa (sandy woods sedge)
Carex debilis (white-edge sedge)
Carex digitalis (slender woodland sedge)
Carex elliottii (Elliott's sedge)
Carex fissa var. *aristata* (hammock sedge)
Carex frankii (Frank's sedge)
Carex gholsonii (Gholson's sedge)
Carex gigantean (giant sedge)
Carex glaucescens (clustered sedge)
Carex hyalinolepis (shoreline sedge)
Carex intumescens (greater bladder sedge)
Carex joorii (cypress swamp sedge)
Carex leptalea (bristly-stalked sedge)
Carex longii (Long's sedge)
Carex lupuliformis (false hop sedge)
Carex lurida (shallow sedge)
Carex nigromarginata var. *floridana* (blackedge sedge)
Carex oxylepis (sharp-scale sedge)
Carex paeninsulae (peninsula sedge)

Carex retroflexa (reflexed sedge)
Carex stipata (awl-fruit sedge)
Carex striata (Walter's sedge)
Carex styloflexa (bent sedge)
Carex tribuloides (blunt broom sedge)
Carex verrucosa (warty sedge)
Carex vexans (Florida hammock sedge)

Dusted Skipper (*Atrytonopsis hianna*)

Poaceae
(grass family)

Andropogon arctatus (pinewoods bluestem)
Andropogon brachystachyus (short spike bluestem)
Andropogon floridanus (Florida bluestem)
Andropogon gerardii (big bluestem)
Andropogon glomeratus (blushy bluestem)
Andropogon gyrans (Elliott's bluestem)
Andropogon longiberbis (hairy bluestem)
Andropogon ternarius (split-beard bluestem)
Andropogon tracyi (Tracy's bluestem)
Andropogon virginicus var. *decipiens* (broom sedge bluestem)
Andropogon virginicus var. *glaucus* (chalky bluestem)

Eufala Skipper (*Lerodea eufala*)

Poaceae
(grass family)

Saccharum alopecuroides (silver plumegrass)
Saccharum baldwinii (narrow plumegrass)
Saccharum giganteum (sugarcane plumegrass)

Fiery Skipper (*Hylephila phyleus*)

Poaceae

(grass family)

Digitaria ciliaris (southern crabgrass)
Digitaria cognata (Carolina crabgrass)
Digitaria filiformis var. *filiformis* (slender crabgrass)
Digitaria floridana (Florida crabgrass)
Digitaria gracillima (longleaf crabgrass)
Digitaria horizontalis (Jamaican crabgrass)
Digitaria insularis (sourgrass)
Digitaria serotina (dwarf crabgrass)
Digitaria simpsonii (Simpson's crabgrass)

Least Skipper (*Ancyloxypha numitor*)

Poaceae

(grass family)

Leersia hexandra (southern cutgrass)
Leersia monandra (bunch cutgrass)
Leersia virginica (white grass)
Zizaniopsis miliacea (southern wild rice)

Meske's Skipper (*Hesperia meskei*)

Poaceae

(grass family)

Andropogon arctatus (pinewoods bluestem)

Andropogon brachystachyus (short spike bluestem)
Andropogon floridanus (Florida bluestem)
Andropogon gerardii (big bluestem)
Andropogon glomeratus (blushy bluestem)
Andropogon gyrans (Elliott's bluestem)
Andropogon longiberbis (hairy bluestem)
Andropogon ternarius (split-beard bluestem)
Andropogon tracyi (Tracy's bluestem)
Andropogon virginicus var. *decipiens* (broom sedge bluestem)
Andropogon virginicus var. *glaucus* (chalky bluestem)
Andropogon virginicus var. *virginicus* (broom sedge bluestem)
Aristida condensata (big threeawn)
Aristida gyrans (corkscrew threeawn)
Aristida lanosa (woolysheath threeawn)
Aristida longespica var. *geniculata* (red threeawn)
Aristida longespica var. *longespica* (slimspike threeawn)
Aristida mohrii (Mohr's threeawn)
Aristida palustris (longleaf threeawn)
Aristida patula (tall threeawn)
Aristida purpurascens var. *purpurascens* (arrowfeather threeawn)
Aristida purpurascens var. *tenuispica* (Hillsboro threeawn)
Aristida purpurascens var. *virgata* (arrowfeather threeawn)
Aristida rhizomophora (Florida threeawn)
Aristida spiciformis (bottlebrush threeawn)
Aristida stricta (wiregrass)

Monk Skipper (*Asboliscapucinus*)

Arecaceae

(palm family)

Rhapidophyllum hystrix (needle palm)
Sabal etonia (scrub palmetto)
Sabal minor (blue-stem palmetto)
Sabal palmetto (cabbage palm)
Serenoa repens (saw palmetto)

Ocola Skipper (*Panoquina ocola*)

Poaceae
(grass family)

Panicum amarum (bitter panicum)
Panicum dichotomiflorum var. *bartowense* (fall panicgrass)
Panicum hemitomom (maidencane)
Panicum virgatum (switchgrass)

Obscure Skipper (*Panoquina panoquinaoides*)

Poaceae
(grass family)

Sporobolus compositus (rough dropseed)
Sporobolus curtissii (Curtiss' dropseed)
Sporobolus domingensis (coral dropseed)
Sporobolus floridanus (Florida dropseed)
Sporobolus junceus (pineywoods dropseed)
Sporobolus virginicus (seashore dropseed)

Palatka Skipper (*Euphyes pilatka*)

Cyperaceae
(sedge family)

Cladium jamaicense (Jamaica swamp sawgrass)

Palmetto Skipper (*Euphyes arpa*)

Arecaceae

(palm family)

Serenoa repens (saw palmetto)

Sachem Skipper (*Atalopedes campestris*)

Poaceae

(grass family)

Digitaria ciliaris (southern crabgrass)
Digitaria cognata (Carolina crabgrass)
Digitaria filiformis var. filiformis (slender crabgrass)
Digitaria floridana (Florida crabgrass)
Digitaria gracillima (longleaf crabgrass)
Digitaria horizontalis (Jamaican crabgrass)
Digitaria insularis (sourgrass)
Digitaria serotina (dwarf crabgrass)
Digitaria simpsonii (Simpson's crabgrass)
Stenotaphrum secundatum (St. Augustine grass)

Saltmarsh Skipper (*Panoquina panoquin*)

Poaceae

(grass family)

Spartina alterniflora (saltmarsh cordgrass)
Spartina bakeri (sand cordgrass)
Spartina cynosuroides (big cordgrass)
Spartina patens (marsh-hay cordgrass)
Spartina spartinae (gulf cordgrass)

Southern Broken-dash (*Wallengrenia otho*)

Poaceae
(grass family)

Paspalum bifidum (pitchfork crowngrass)
Paspalum boscianum (bull crowngrass)
Paspalum botterii (rustyseed paspalum)
Paspalum caespitosum (blue crowngrass)
Paspalum conjugatum (sour paspalum)
Paspalum dissectum (mudbank crowngrass)
Paspalum distichum (knotgrass)
Paspalum eglume (Florida reimargrass)
Paspalum floridanum (Florida paspalum)
Paspalum leave (field paspalum)
Paspalum plicatulum (brownseed paspalum)
Paspalum praecox (early paspalum)
Paspalum pubiflorum (hairyseed paspalum)
Paspalum repens (water paspalum)
Paspalum setaceum (thin paspalum)
Paspalum vaginatum (seashore paspalum)
Stenotaphrum secundatum (St. Augustine grass)

Southern Skipperling (*Copaeodes minima*)

Poaceae
(grass family)

grasses
(no specific species documented)

Swarthy Skipper (*Nastra lherminier*)

Poaceae

(grass family)

Andropogon arctatus (pinewoods bluestem)
Andropogon brachystachyus (short spike bluestem)
Andropogon floridanus (Florida bluestem)
Andropogon gerardii (big bluestem)
Andropogon glomeratus (blushy bluestem)
Andropogon gyrans (Elliott's bluestem)
Andropogon longiberbis (hairy bluestem)
Andropogon ternarius (split-beard bluestem)
Andropogon tracyi (Tracy's bluestem)
Andropogon virginicus var. *decipiens* (broom sedge bluestem)
Andropogon virginicus var. *glaucus* (chalky bluestem)
Andropogon virginicus var. *virginicus* (broom sedge bluestem)

Tawny-edged Skipper (*Polites themistocles*)

Poaceae

(grass family)

Panicum amarum (bitter panicum)
Panicum dichotomiflorum var. *bartowense* (fall panicgrass)
Panicum hemitomom (maidencane)
Panicum virgatum (switchgrass)

Twin-spot Skipper (*Oligoria maculata*)

Poaceae

(grass family)

Andropogon arctatus (pinewoods bluestem)
Andropogon brachystachyus (short spike bluestem)
Andropogon floridanus (Florida bluestem)

Andropogon gerardii (big bluestem)
Andropogon glomeratus (blushy bluestem)
Andropogon gyrans (Elliott's bluestem)
Andropogon longiberbis (hairy bluestem)
Andropogon ternarius (split-beard bluestem)
Andropogon tracyi (Tracy's bluestem)
Andropogon virginicus var. *decipiens* (broom sedge bluestem)
Andropogon virginicus var. *glaucus* (chalky bluestem)
Andropogon virginicus var. *virginicus* (broom sedge bluestem)

Whirlabout skipper (*Polites vibex*)

Poaceae
(grass family)

Paspalum bifidum (pitchfork crowngrass)
Paspalum boscianum (bull crowngrass)
Paspalum botterii (rustyseed paspalum)
Paspalum caespitosum (blue crowngrass)
Paspalum conjugatum (sour paspalum)
Paspalum dissectum (mudbank crowngrass)
Paspalum distichum (knotgrass)
Paspalum eglume (Florida reimargrass)
Paspalum floridanum (Florida paspalum)
Paspalum leave (field paspalum)
Paspalum plicatulum (brownseed paspalum)
Paspalum praecox (early paspalum)
Paspalum pubiflorum (hairyseed paspalum)
Paspalum repens (water paspalum)
Paspalum setaceum (thin paspalum)
Paspalum vaginatum (seashore paspalum)

Stenotaphrum secundatum (St. Augustine grass)

Section 24

Giant Skipper Butterflies and Their Host Plants

Cofaqui Giant Skipper (*Megathymus cofaqui*)

Agavaceae
(agave family)

Yucca aloifolia (Spanish bayonet)
Yucca filamentosa (Adam's needle)
Yucca gloriosa (mound-lily yucca)

Yucca Giant Skipper (*Megathymus yuccae*)

Agavaceae
(agave family)

Yucca aloifolia (Spanish bayonet)
Yucca filamentosa (Adam's needle)
Yucca gloriosa (mound-lily yucca)

Native Nectar Sources: Wildflowers

Butterflies have relatively short tongues so they need short flowers in order to reach the nectar and feed. You will usually notice, with exceptions, butterflies visiting flowers that are matched to their size. Large butterflies are physically able to access the nectar reserves in larger flowers, but generally not the long tubular shapes frequented by hummingbirds. They can use most morning glories; it's really an issue of what is comfortable for them. Small flowers tend to be visited by small butterflies like skippers and crescents.

Butterflies do not hover like hummingbirds so they search for flowers with a landing area, or at least a place where they can occasionally grasp with their feet for support while feeding. Also, if the flower tube is too short large butterflies find feeding uncomfortable.

Following are nectar plant charts that will help guide you in selecting central Florida native plant nectar sources. Many flowering plants were left out merely because butterflies cannot reach the nectar and therefore seldom use them. So, most of my choices are geared towards usability.

Latin Name	Common Name	Flower Color	Bloom Time	Height	Light	Water
Ageratina jucunda	hammock snakeroot	white	sum-fall	3'	pt sh-sun	avg-dry
Amorpha herbacea	white indigo	white	spring	3'	sun	avg-dry
Asclepias incarnata	swamp milkweed	pink	sp,su,fa	3'	sun	avg-moist
Asclepias perennis	swamp milkweed	white	all year	2'	pt sh-sun	avg-moist
Asclepias tuberosa	butterfly milkweed	orange	sp,su,fa	3'	sun	avg-dry
Balduina angustifolia	yellow buttons	yellow	sp,su,fa	3'	sun	avg-dry

Latin Name	Common Name	Flower Color	Bloom Time	Height	Light	Water
Bidens alba	beggarticks	white	all year	3'	pt sh-sun	avg
Carphephorus corymbosus	Florida paintbrush	pink	sum-fall	3'	sun	avg-dry
Ceanothus microphyllus	littleleaf buckbrush	white	spring	2'	pt sh-sun	avg-dry
Cicuta maculata	water hemlock	white	sp,su,fa	3'	pt sh-sun	moist-wet
Cnidoscolus stimulosus	tread softly	white	all year	3'	pt sh-sun	avg-dry
Dalea pinnata	summer farewell	white	sum-fall	3'	pt sh-sun	avg-dry
Elephantopus elata	elephant's foot	lilac	sum-fall	3'	pt sh-sun	avg-dry
Erigeron quercifolius	southern fleabane	white	spring	2'	pt sh-sun	avg-dry
Erigeron strigosus	daisy fleabane	white	spring	2'	pt sh-sun	avg-dry
Eriogonum tomentosa	wild buckwheat	white	all year	3'	pt sh-sun	avg-dry
Eupatorium perfoliatum	common boneset	white	sp-sum	5'	pt sh-sun	moist-wet
Gaillardia pulchella	blanket flower	orange	all year	2'	sun	avg-dry
Garberia heterophylla	garberia	lilac	sum-fall	6'	pt sh-sun	avg-dry
Glandularia tampensis	Tampa vervain	pink	sp,su,fa	2'	pt sh-sun	avg-moist
Heliotropium curassavicum	seaside heliotrope	white	all year	3'	sun	avg-dry
Heliotropoum polyphyullum	pineland heliotrope	white	all year	3'	sun	avg-dry

Latin Name	Common Name	Flower Color	Bloom Time	Height	Light	Water
Hyptis alata	musky mint	white	all year	6'	pt sh-sun	avg-moist
Iponopsis rubra	standing cypress	red	sum-fall	3'	sun	avg-dry
Lachnanthes caroliniana	redroot	green	sp,su,fa	3'	pt sh-sun	moist-wet
Liatris gracilis	graceful blazing star	pink	sum-fall	3'	pt sh-sun	avg-dry
Lobelia cardinalis	cardinal flower	red	sum-fall	6'	pt sh-sun	moist-wet
Oclemena reticulata	white topped aster	white	all year	3'	pt sh-sun	avg-moist
Oenothera simulans	southern beeblossom	blush	all year	5'	sun	avg-dry
Melanthera nivea	snow squarestem	white	sum-fall	6'	pt sh-sun	avg-moist
Palafoxia integrifolia	coastalplain palafox	blush	sum-fall	4'	pt sh-sun	avg-dry
Penstemon multiflorus	beardtongue	white	sp-sum	3'	pt sh-sun	avg-dry
Piloblephis rigida	false pennyroyal	lilac	spring	1'	sun	avg-dry
Polygonella fimbriata	sandhill wireweed	blush	sum-fall	3'	pt sh-sun	avg-dry
Ruella caroliniensis	wild petunia	blue	sp,su,fa	2'	pt sh-sun	avg
Salvia coccinea	red salvia	red	all year	3'	pt sh-sun	avg
Salvia lyrata	lyre-leaf sage	blue	spring	2'	pt sh-sun	avg
Saururus cernuus	lizard's tail	white	sp-sum	3'	pt sh-sun	moist-wet

Latin Name	Common Name	Flower Color	Bloom Time	Height	Light	Water
Sabatia brevifolia	shortleaf rose gentian	pink	sp-sum	2'	pt sh-sun	moist-wet
Stachytarpheta jamaicensis	porterweed	blue	all year	3'	sun	avg
Stokesia laevis	Stoke's aster	purple	sp,su,fa	2'	sun	avg-moist
Verbesina virginica	frostweed	white	sum-fall	6'	pt sh-sun	avg
Verbesina angustifolia	ironweed	purple	sum-fall	4'	pt sh-sun	avg
Vernonia gigantea	giant ironweed	purple	sum-fall	6'	pt sh-sun	avg

Native Nectar Sources: Trees

Latin name	Common Name	Flower Color	Bloom Time	Height	Light	Water
Aralia spinosa	devil's walking stick	green	summer	30'	pt sh-su	avg
Cartrema americanum	wild olive	green	spring	50'	pt shade	dry-moist
Cercis canadensis	red bud	pink	spring	25'	pt shade	avg-moist
Cliftonia monophylla	black titi	white	spring	24'	pt sh-su	avg-moist
Coccoloba uvifera	sea grape	white	spring	50'	sun	avg-dry
Crataegus marshallii	parsley haw	white	spring	15'	pt sh-su	avg-dry
Crataegus michauxii	Michaux's hawthorn	white	spring	15'	pt sh-su	avg-dry
Eugenia axillaris	white stopper	white	sp-sum	25'	pt sh-su	avg-dry
Eugenia foetida	Spanish stopper	white	sp-sum	20'	pt sh-su	avg-dry
Gordonia Lasianthus	loblolly bay	white	sum-fall	40'	pt sh-su	avg-moist
Ilex ambigua	Carolina holly	white	spring	18'	pt shade	avg-dry
Ilex cassine	dahoon holly	white	sp,su,w	30'	pt shade	avg-dry
Ilex glabra	gallberry	white	sp,su,w	8'	pt sh-su	avg-moist

Ilex vomitoria	yaupon holly	white	spring	25'	pt sh-su	avg-moist
Myrcianthes fragrans	Simpson stopper	white	sp-sum	20'	pt sh-su	avg-dry
Oxydendrum arboreum	sourwood	white	summer	35-70'	pt shade	avg-dry
Pinckneya bracteata	fevertree	pink	summer	15-30'	pt shade	avg-wet
Prunus americana	American plum	white	spring	20'	pt sh-su	avg-dry
Prunus angustifolia	chickasaw plum	white	spring	25'	pt sh-su	avg-dry
Prunus caroliniana	cherry laurel	white	spring	30'	pt sh-su	avg
Prunus serotina	black cherry	white	spring	60'	pt sh-su	avg-moist
Prunus umbellata	flatwoods plum	white	spring	15-35'	pt sh-su	avg-dry
Rhus copallinum	winged sumac	yellow	sp-sum	20'	pt shade	avg-dry
Sideroxylon tenax	tough bully	white	summer	15'	pt sh-su	avg-dry
Symplocos tinctoria	horse sugar	yellow	spring	15'	pt sh-su	avg-moist
Vaccinium arboreum	sparkleberry	white	spring	25'	pt shade	avg-dry
Zanthoxylum clava-hercules	Hercule's club	green	spring	50'	pt sh-su	avg-moist

Native Nector Sources: Shrubs

Latin Name	Common Name	Flower Color	Bloom Time	Height	Light	Water
Amorpha fruticosa	bastard false indigo	maroon	sp-sum	10'	pt sh-sun	avg-dry
Aronia arbutifolia	red chokeberry	white	spring	10'	pt sh-sun	avg-moist
Bejaria racemosa	tarflower	pink	sp-sum	8'	pt sh-sun	dry
Ceanothus americanus	New Jersey tea	white	sum-fall	2'	pt sh-sun	avg-dry
Ceonothus microphyllus	littleaf buckbrush	white	spring	1'	pt shade	avg-dry
Cephalanthus occidentalis	buttonbush	white	sp,su,fa	10'	pt sh-sun	avg-dry
Clethra alnifolia	sweet pepperbush	white	summer	5'	pt sh-sun	moist-wet
Cliftonia monophylla	black titi	white	spring	10'	pt sh-sun	moist-wet
Cordia globosa	bloodberry	white	sp,su,fa	5'	pt sh-sun	avg
Decodon verticillatus	swamp loosestrife	pink	sum-fall	3'	sun	moist-wet
Ernodea littoralis	beach creeper	orange	all year	2'	sun	avg-dry
Erythrina herbacea	coral bean	red	sp-sum	4'	pt sh-sun	avg-dry
Garberia	garberia	lilac	sum-	6'	pt sh-	avg-dry

heterophylla			fall		sun		
Hamelia patens	firebush	red	all year	15'	pt sh-sun	avg	
Hibiscus aculeatus	comfort-root	cream	sum-fall	4'	pt sh-sun	avg-dry	
Hibiscus coccineus	scarlet hibiscus	red	sum-fall	5'	pt sh-sun	avg-moist	
Hibiscus grandiflorus	swamp rose-mallow	pink	sum-fall	5'	pt sh-sun	avg-moist	
Hibiscus moscheutos	rosemallow	cream	sum-fall	4'	pt sh-sun	moist-wet	
Hydrangea quercifolia	oakleaf hydrangea	white	summer	10-15'	pt shade	avg-moist	
Itea virginica	Virginia willow	white	sp-sum	3'	pt shade	avg-moist	
Lantana involucrata	buttonsage	white	all year	1-3'	pt sh-sun	avg-dry	
Lantana depressa	pineland lantana	yellow	all year	1-2'	pt sh-sun	avg-dry	
Quadrella jamaicensis	jamaican caper tree	white	sp-sum	6-10'	pt sh-sun	avg-dry	
Rhododendron canescens	wild azelia	pink	spring	6-8'	pt shade	avg-moist	
Rubus cuneifolius	sand blackberry	white	sp-sum	3'	pt sh-sun	dry	
Rubus trivialis	southern dewberry	white	sp-sum	5'	pt sh-sun	avg-moist	
Viburnum dentatum	arrowwood	white	sp-sum	6-12'	pt sh-sun	avg-moist	
Viburnum obovatum	Walter's viburnum	white	spring	12-36'	pt sh-sun	avg-moist	
Viburnum nudum	possumhaw	white	summer	12-36'	pt sh-sun	avg-moist	

Native Nectar Sources: Vines

Latin Name	Common Name	Flower Color	Bloom Time	Length	Light	Water
Ampelaster carolinianus	climbing aster	lilac	fall	6'	pt sh-sun	avg-moist
Canavalia rosea	beach bean	pink	sum-fall	20'	sun	avg-dry
Centrosema virginianum	spurred butterfly pea	lilac	summer	10'	pt sh-sun	avg-dry
Clematis virginiana	virgin's bower	white	summer	20'	pt sh-sun	dry-moist
Clitoria mariana	Atlantic pigeonwings	lilac	summer	6'	pt sh-sun	avg-dry
Cynanchum laeve	honeyvine	white	sum-fall	15'	pt sh-sun	dry-moist
Echites umbellata	rubber vine	white	all year	15'	pt sh-sun	dry
Funastrum clausum	white twinevine	white	all year	20'	pt sh-sun	avg-moist
Galactia floridana	Florida milkpea	pink	all year	3'	pt sh-sun	avg-dry
Galactia volubilis	eastern milkpea	pink	sum-fall	4'	pt sh-sun	avg-dry
Hydrangea barbara	climbing hydrangea	white	sp,su,fa	30'	pt shade	avg-moist
Ipomoea cordatotriloba	tievine moring glory	pink	sp,su,fa	20'	pt sh-sun	avg
Ipomoea	scarlet	red	sp,su,f	20'	pt sh-	avg

hederifolia	morning glory		a			sun	
Ipomoea imperati	beach morning glory	white	sum-fall	30'		sun	avg-dry
Ipomoea indica	ocean blue morning glory	blue	sp,su,fa	30'		sun	avg-dry
Ipomoea lacunosa	whitestar	white	sum-fall	10'		sun	avg-moist
Ipomoea pandurata	man-of-the-earth	white	summer	30'		pt sh-sun	dry-moist
Ipomoea pes-caprae	railroad vine	pink	all year	20'		sun	avg-dry
Ipomoea sagittata	saltmarsh morning glory	pink	all year	8'		sun	moist-wet
Lonicera sempervirens	coral honeysuckle	red	sp-sum	15'		pt sh-sun	avg-dry
Mikania scandens	climbing hempvine	white	summer	15'		pt shade	avg-moist
Wisteria frutescens	American wisteria	lilac	summer	30'		pt sh-sun	avg-moist

Bibliography

Ajilvsgi, Geyata. *Butterfly Gardening for the South*. Taylor Publishing: Dallas, TX. 1990

Bell and Taylor. *Florida Wildflowers and Roadside Plants*. Laurel Hill Press: Chapel Hill, NC. 1982

Emmel, Thomas. *Florida's Fabulous Butterflies*. World Publications: Tampa, FL. 1997

Glassberg, J. et al. *Butterflies Through Binoculars: Florida*. Oxford University Press 2000

Huegel, C. *Butterfly Gardening with Florida's Native Plants*. Florida Native Plant Society: Orlando, FL. 1992

Huegel, Craig N. *Florida Plants for Wildlife*. The Florida Native Plant Society. 1995

Lady Bird Johnson Wildflower Center (https://www.wildflower.org/plants/). The University of Texas at Austin. https://www.wildflower.org/plants/

Lotts, Kelly and Thomas Naberhaus, coordinators. 2017. Butterflies and Moths of North America (https://www.butterfliesandmoths.org/). http://www.butterfliesandmoths.org/

Minno, Marc & Maria. *Florida Butterfly Gardening: A Complete Guide to Attracting, Identifying, and Enjoying Butterflies*. University Press of Florida: Gainesville, FL. 1999

Nelson, Gil. *The Shrubs & Woody Vines of Florida*. Pineapple Press: Sarasota, FL 1996

Nelson, Gil. *The Trees of Florida*. Pineapple Press: Sarasota, FL 1994

Pyle, Robert Michael. *The National Audubon Society Field Guide to North American Butterflies*. Knopf. 1981

Taylor, Walter K. *The Guide to Florida Wildflowers*. Taylor Publishing: Dallas, TX 1992

Wasowski, Sally. *Gardening with Native Plants of the South*. Taylor Publishing: Dallas, TX 1994

Wunderlin, Richard *Guide to the Vascular Plants of Central Florida*. University Press of FL: Gainesville, FL. 1998

Index

A

Aaron's skipper, 68
Abaeis nicippe, 36
Acanthaceae, 54
Acanthus family, 54
Adam's needle, 80
Aeschynomene americana, 34
Aeschynomene pratensis, 34
Aeschynomene viscidula, 34
Agalinis divaricata, 50
Agalinis fasciculata, 50
Agalinis filicaulis, 50
Agalinis filifolia, 50
Agalinis harperi, 50
Agalinis laxa, 50
Agalinis linifolia, 50
Agalinis maritima, 50
Agalinis obtusifolia, 51
Agalinis plukenetii, 51
Agalinis purpurea, 51
Agalinis setacea, 51
Agalinis tenuifolia, 51
Agavaceae, 80
agave family, 80
Agraulis vanilla, 48
alligator flag, 69
amaranth family, 39, 62
Amaranthaceae, 39, 62
American bluehearts, 51
American elm, 53
American lady, 50
American searocket, 32, 33
American snout, 43
American wild carrot, 28
Americanum, 29, 86
Amorpha fruticosa, 36, 63
Amorpha herbacea, 36
Amorpha herbacea var. *herbacea*, 63
Amyris elemifera, 29
Anacardiaceae, 42
Anaea troglodyte floridalis, 51
Anartia jatrophae, 15, 55
Anatrytone logan, 70
Ancyloxypha numitor, 74

Andropogon arctatus, 72, 73, 78
Andropogon brachystachyus, 72, 74, 78
Andropogon floridanus, 72, 74, 78
Andropogon gerardii, 72, 74, 78, 79
Andropogon glomeratus, 72, 74, 78, 79
Andropogon gyrans, 72, 74, 78, 79
Andropogon longiberbis, 72, 74, 78, 79
Andropogon ternarius, 72, 74, 78, 79
Andropogon tracyi, 72, 74, 78, 79
Andropogon virginicus var. *decipiens,* 72, 74, 78, 79
Andropogon virginicus var. *glaucus,* 72, 74, 78, 79
Andropogon virginicus var. *virginicus,* 72, 74, 78, 79
Annona glabra, 31
Annonaceae, 30
annual glasswort, 39
Anthanassa texana, 54
Apalachicola toadflax, 51
Apiaceae, 28
Apocynaceae, 45, 46
Appalachian brown, 57
Arecaceae, 74, 76
Aristida condensata, 74
Aristida gyrans, 74
Aristida lanosa, 74
Aristida longespica var. *geniculata,* 74
Aristida longespica var. *longespica,* 74
Aristida mohrii, 74
Aristida palustris, 74
Aristida patula, 74
Aristida purpurascens var. *purpurascens,* 74
Aristida purpurascens var. *tenuispica,* 74
Aristida purpurascens var. *virgata,* 74
Aristida rhizomophora, 74
Aristida spiciformis, 74
Aristida stricta, 74
Aristolochia serpentaria, 29, 30
Aristolochia tomentosa, 17, 29, 30
Aristolochiaceae, 29, 30
Arogos skipper, 69
arrow root family, 70
arrowfeather threeawn, 74
Artemisia campestris subsp. *Caudata,* 50
Arundinaria gigantea, 60
Asbolis capucinus, 74
Ascia monuste, 33
Asclepias amplexicaulis, 45, 46
Asclepias cinerea, 45, 46
Asclepias connivens, 45, 46

Asclepias curtissii, 45, 46
Asclepias feayi, 45, 46
Asclepias humistrata, 26, 45, 46, 47
Asclepias incarnata, 45, 46, 47, 81
Asclepias lanceolata, 45, 46, 47
Asclepias longifolia, 45, 46, 47
Asclepias pedicellata, 45, 46, 47
Asclepias perennis, 45, 46, 47, 82
Asclepias tomentosa, 45, 46, 47
Asclepias tuberosa, 45, 46, 47
Asclepias verticillata, 45, 46, 47
Asclepias viridis, 45, 46, 47
Asclepias viridula, 45, 46, 47
Asimina angustifolia, 31
Asimina incana, 31
Asimina manasota, 31
Asimina obovata, 31
Asimina parviflora, 31
Asimina pulchella, 31
Asimina pygmea, 31
Asimina reticulata, 31
Aster Family, 35, 50, 51, 52, 56
Asteraceae, 35, 50, 51, 52, 56
Asterocampa celtis, 43
Asterocampa clyton, 43
Atalopedes campestris, 76
Atlantic pigeon-wings, 62
Atlides halesus, 40
Atrytone arogos, 69
Atrytonopsis hianna, 72
awl-fruit sedge, 58, 72

B

Bacopa caroliniana, 55
Bacopa innominata, 55
Bacopa monnieri, 55
Bahama aster, 52
Baldwin's eryngo, 28
bandanna of the Everglades, 69
banded hairstreak, 39
baracoa skipper, 69
barred yellow, 34
bastard false indigo, 36, 63, 87
Battus philenor, 17, 29
Battus polydamas, 30
bayberry family, 41
bayleaf capertree, 32, 33
beach croton, 51

beach false foxglove, 50
beggarticks, 35, 83
bent sedge, 58, 73
Bidens alba, 35, 83
Bidens bipinnata, 35
Bidens laevis, 35
Bidens mitis, 35
big bluestem, 74, 79
big cordgrass, 76
big threeawn, 74
bigflower pawpaw, 31
birthwort family, 29, 30
bitter panicum, 68, 70, 75, 78
black cherry, 18, 24, 54, 86
black swallowtail, 18, 28
blackedge sedge, 58, 71
blue crown-grass, 58
blue crowngrass, 79
blue sedge, 57, 71
blue-stem palmetto, 74
bluejack oak, 39, 41, 42, 65, 66, 67
blunt broom sedge, 58, 72
blushy bluestem, 74, 78
Boehmeria cylindrica, 53
bog white violet, 48
bottlebrush threeawn, 74
bracted fan-petals, 65, 67
Brassicaeae, 32, 33
Brephidium pseudofea, 38
bristly scaleseed, 28
bristly-stalked sedge, 57, 71
broadleaf signal-grass, 58
broadwing sedge, 57, 71
brome-like sedge, 57, 71
broom sedge bluestem, 72, 74, 78, 79
broom-rape family, 50
brown seed paspalum, 58
Buchnera americana, 51
buckeye, 50
buffalo clover, 36
bull crown-grass, 58
bull crowngrass, 77, 79
bunch cutgrass, 74
butterfly milkweed, 45, 46, 47, 81
button rattlesnakemaster, 28
byssus skipper, 69

C

cabbage palm, 75
cabbage white, 32
Cakile edentula, 32, 33
Calephelis virginiensis, 56
Calpodes ethlius, 69
Calycopis cecrops, 41
Canada toadflax, 51
Canadian blacksnakeroot, 28
Canadian honewort, 28
canna family, 69
Canna flaccida, 69
canna skipper, 69
Cannaceae, 69
Cardamine bulbosa, 32, 33
Carex alata, 57, 71
Carex atlantica subsp. *Capillacea*, 57, 71
Carex basiantha, 57, 71
Carex blanda, 57, 71
Carex bromoides, 57, 71
Carex chapmannii, 57, 71
Carex cherokeensis, 57, 71
Carex comosa, 57, 71
Carex complanata, 57, 71
Carex crebriflora, 57, 71
Carex crus-corvi, 57, 71
Carex dasycarpa, 57, 71
Carex debilis, 57, 71
Carex digitalis, 57, 71
Carex elliottii, 57, 71
Carex fissa var. *aristata*, 57, 71
Carex frankii, 57, 71
Carex gholsonii, 57, 71
Carex gigantean, 57, 71
Carex glaucescens, 57, 71
Carex hyalinolepis, 57, 71
Carex intumescens, 57, 71
Carex joorii, 57, 71
Carex leptalea, 57, 71
Carex longii, 57, 71
Carex lupuliformis, 58, 71
Carex lurida, 58, 71
Carex nigromarginata var. *floridana*, 58, 71
Carex oxylepis, 58, 71
Carex paeninsulae, 58, 71
Carex retroflexa, 58, 72
Carex stipata, 58, 72
Carex striata, 58, 72
Carex styloflexa, 58, 72
Carex tribuloides, 58, 72

Carex verrucosa, 58, 72
Carex vexans, 58, 72
Carolina basswood, 53
Carolina clover, 36
Carolina crabgrass, 71, 73, 76
Carolina fluff grass, 59
Carolina grasswort, 28
Carolina milkweed, 45, 46
Carolina Satyr, 58
Carolina violet, 48
Carya aquatica, 39
Carya floridana, 39
Carya glabra, 39
Carya tomentosa, 39
cassius blue, 38
Cassytha filiformis, 29, 30
cat claw blackbead, 35
cedar elm, 53
celery family, 28
Celtis, 43, 52
Celtis iguanaea, 43, 52
Celtis laevigata, 43, 52
Centrosema arenicola, 38, 62
Centrosema virginianum, 38, 62, 89
ceraunus blue, 38
Cercyonis pegala, 59
Chaerophyllum tainturieri, 28
chalky bluestem, 72, 74, 78, 79
Chamaecrista fasciculata, 35
Chamaecrista nictitans, 35
Chapman's oak, 39, 41, 42, 65, 66, 67
Chapman's sedge, 57, 72
Chasmanthium laxum, 58, 59
Chasmanthium nitidum, 58, 59
Chasmanthium sessiliflorum, 58, 59
checkered skipper, 65, 67
checkered white, 32
cheesytoes, 34
Cherokee sedge, 57, 71
cherry laurel, 54, 86
chickasaw plum, 54, 86
Cicuta maculata, 28, 82
Cirsium horridulum, 51, 56
Cirsium muticum, 56
Cirsium nuttallii, 51, 56
citrus family, 29
Cladium jamaicense, 75
clasping milkweed, 45, 46
climbing aster, 52, 89

Clitoria fragrans, 62
Clitoria mariana, 62
clouded skipper, 70
cloudless sulphur, 20, 34, 44
clustered pellitory, 53
clustered sedge, 57, 72
clusterspike false indigo, 36, 63
coastal plain sedge, 57, 72
coastal plain willow, 54, 55
cockspur hawthorn, 42
cofaqui giant skipper, 81
Colias eurytheme, 36
common blue violet, 48
common fan-petals, 65, 67
common wood nymph, 59
confused cloudywing, 61
Cooley's water willow, 54
Copaeodes minima, 78
coral dropseed, 76
corkscrew threeawn, 75
corkystem passionflower, 48, 49
corkystem passionvine, 8
Crataegus aestivalis, 42
Crataegus crus-galli, 42
Crataegus marshallii, 42
Crataegus michauxii, 42
Crataegus uniflora, 42
Crataegus viridis, 42
creeping eryngo, 28
Croton argyranthemus, 51
Croton capitatus, 51
Croton glandulosus, 51
Croton michauxii, 51
Croton punctatus, 51
Cryptotaenia canadensis, 28
Curtiss' dropseed, 76
Curtiss' milkweed, 45, 46, 47
custard apple family, 31
Cyllopsis gemma, 59
Cynanchum northropiae, 45, 46, 47
Cynophalla flexuosa, 32, 33
Cyperaceae, 57, 71, 75
cypress swamp sedge, 57, 71

D

dainty sulphur, 34
Dalea adenopoda, 36
Dalea carnea var. *albida*, 36

Dalea carnea var. *carnea*, 36
Dalea feayi, 36
Dalea pinnata, 36
Danaus eresimus, 46
Danaus gilippus, 46
Danaus plexippus, 26, 45
Daucus pusillus, 28
Delaware skipper, 71
delicate everlasting, 50
Desmodium canescens, 40, 61, 62, 63, 64
Desmodium ciliare, 40, 61, 62, 63, 64
Desmodium floridanum, 40, 61, 62, 63, 64
Desmodium glabellum, 40, 61, 62, 63, 64
Desmodium paniculatum, 40, 61, 62, 63, 64
Desmodium perplexum, 40, 61, 62, 63, 64
Desmodium strictum, 40, 61, 62, 63, 64
Desmodium tenuifolium, 40, 61, 62, 63, 64
Desmodium viridiflorum, 40, 61, 62, 63, 64
Digitaria ciliaris, 70, 73, 76
Digitaria cognata, 70, 73, 76
Digitaria filiformis var. *filiformis*, 70, 73, 76
Digitaria floridana, 70, 73, 76
Digitaria gracillima, 70, 73, 76
Digitaria horizontalis, 70, 73, 76
Digitaria insularis, 70, 73, 76
Digitaria serotina, 70, 73, 76
Digitaria simpsonii, 70, 73, 76
Dillenius' ticktrefoil, 40, 61, 62, 63, 64
doctorbush, 38
dogbane family, 45, 46
Dominican signal-grass, 58
Dorantes longtail, 61
dotted skipper, 70
dun skipper, 71
dusted skipper, 72
dwarf crabgrass, 70, 73, 76
dwarf hawthorn, 42
dwarf live oak, 39, 40, 41, 65, 66, 67
dwarf nettle, 53
dwarf pawpaw, 31

E

early blue violet, 48
early paspalum, 58, 77, 79
eastern cottonwood, 54
eastern gamagrass, 69
eastern grasswort, 28
eastern milkpea, 10, 38, 40, 89

eastern pygmy blue, 38
eastern silver aster, 52
eastern woodland sedge, 57, 71
Elliott's aster, 52
Elliott's bluestem, 72, 74, 78
Elliott's fan-petals, 65, 67
Elliott's milkpea, 38, 40
Elliott's sedge, 57, 71
elm family, 53
Enodia portlandia, 60
Epargyreus clarus, 63
Ericaceae, 42
Eryngium aquaticum, 28
Eryngium aromaticum, 28
Eryngium baldwinii, 28
Eryngium prostratum, 28
Eryngium yuccifolium, 28
Erynnis brizo, 66
Erynnis horatius, 65
Erynnis juvenalis, 66
Erynnis zarucco, 67
Eufala skipper, 72
Euphorbiaceae, 51
Euphyes arpa, 76
Euphyes pilatka, 75
Euphyes vestris, 71
Euptoieta claudia, 48
Eurema daira, 34
Eurytides marcellus, 22, 31

F

Fabaceae, 34, 35, 36, 38, 40, 61, 62, 63
Fagaceae, 39, 41, 42, 65, 66, 67
fall panicgrass, 69, 71, 76, 79
false hop sedge, 58, 72
false indigo, 63
false nettle, 53
false tamarind, 35
Feay's prarie clover, 36
few-flower milkweed, 45. 46. 47
field pansy, 48
field paspalum, 58, 78, 80
field wormwood, 50
fiery skipper, 73
flatwoods plum, 54, 86
flaxleaf false foxglove, 50
Florida bluestem, 72, 74, 78
Florida crabgrass, 70, 73, 76

Florida dropseed, 75
Florida hammock sedge, 57, 72
Florida ironweed, 50
Florida leafwing, 51
Florida milkpea, 9, 38, 40, 89
Florida milkvine, 45, 46, 47
Florida milkweed, 45, 46, 47
Florida paspalum, 58, 77, 79
Florida pellitory, 53
Florida reimargrass, 58, 77, 79
Florida threeawn, 74
Florida ticktrefoil, 40, 61, 62, 63, 64
Florida water aster, 52
Florida willow, 54, 55
fragrant eryngo, 28
fragrant swallow-wort, 45, 46, 47
Frank's sedge, 57, 71
fog fruit, 52, 55
Funastrum clausum, 45, 46, 47, 89

G

Galactia elliottii, 38, 40
Galactia floridana, 38, 40, 89
Galactia mollis, 38, 40
Galactia purshii, 38, 40
Galactia volubilis, 10, 38, 40, 89
Gamochaeta antillana, 50
Gamochaeta argyrinea, 50
Gamochaeta purpurea, 50
gemmed satyr, 59
Georgia satyr, 59
Gholson's sedge, 57, 71
giant ironweed, 7, 50, 84
giant sedge, 57, 71
giant swallowtail, 13, 28
golden alexanders, 28
grass family, 58, 59, 60, 69, 70, 71, 72, 73, 74, 76, 77, 78, 79
gray hairstreak, 10, 40
great purple hairstreak, 40
great southern white, 33
greater bladder sedge, 57, 72
green antelope-horn, 45, 46, 47
green hawthorn, 42
green milkweed, 45, 46, 47
gulf cordgrass, 76
gulf fritillary, 48

H

hackberry, 43, 52
hackberry butterfly, 43
hackberry family, 43, 52
hairy bluestem, 72, 74, 78
hairy seed paspalum, 58, 77
hairy small-leaf ticktrefoil, 40, 61, 62, 63, 64
hairyfruit chervil, 28
hairypod cowpea, 38
hammock sedge, 57, 71
Harper's false foxglove, 50
Hayhurst's scallopwing, 62
heartleaf nettle, 53
heath family, 42
Heliconius charithonia, 7, 8, 49
Hemiargus ceraunus, 38
herb-of-grace, 55
Hercule's club, 29, 86
Hermeuptychia sosybius, 58
Hesperia attalus, 70
Hesperia meskei, 73
hickory family, 39
Hillsboro threeawn, 74
hoary ticktrefoil, 41, 61, 62, 63, 64
hoptree, 29
Horace's duskywing, 65
Hylephila phyleus, 73

I

iguana hackberry, 43, 52
Indian hemp, 65, 67
instar, 18, 19, 25
Iresine diffusa, 62

J

Jackson false foxglove, 50
Jamaica swamp sawgrass, 75
Jamaican capertree, 32, 33
Jamaican crabgrass, 70, 73, 76
Juba's bush, 62
Juglandaceae, 39
Junonia coenia, 50
Justicia angusta, 54
Justicia ovata var. *ovata,* 54
Justicia pringlei, 54
Juvenal's duskywing, 66

K

knotgrass, 58, 77, 79
Kosteletzkya pentacarpos, 40

L

Lancewood, 29, 30
large flower milkweed, 45, 46
large orange sulphur, 35
Lauraceae, 29, 30
laurel family, 29, 30
laurel oak, 39, 41, 42, 65, 66, 67
leafless swallow-wort, 45, 46, 47
least skipper, 73
Leersia hexandra, 73
Leersia monandra, 73
Leersia virginica, 73
lemon bacopa, 55
Leptotes cassius, 38
Lerema accius, 69
Lerodea eufala, 72
Libytheana carinenta, 43
Lilaeopsis carolinensis, 28
Lilaeopsis chinensis, 28
lime prickly ash, 29
Limenitis archippus, 54
Limenitis arthemis, 24, 53
Linaria canadensis, 51
Linaria floridana, 51
Lindera benzoin, 29, 30
Liquidambar styraciflua, 15
Liriodendron tulipifera, 30
Litsea aestivalis, 29, 30
little metalmark, 56
little yellow, 35
live oak, 40, 41, 42, 66, 67
long-hair sedge, 57, 71
long-leaf milkweed, 45, 46, 47
long-tailed skipper, 62
longleaf crabgrass, 70, 73, 76
longleaf threeaw, 74
longleaf wood-oats, 58, 59
Long's sedge, 57, 71
loose flower waterwillow, 54

lopsided Indian-grass, 59, 68
love vine, 29, 30
Lysiloma latisiliquum, 35

M

magnolia family, 30
Magnolia grandiflora, 30
Magnolia virginiana, 30
Magnoliaceae, 30
maidencane, 68, 70, 71, 75, 78
mallow family, 40, 53, 65, 67
Malvaceae, 40, 53, 65, 67
Manasota pawpaw, 31
mangrove family, 63
mangrove skipper, 62
Marantaceae, 69
marsh-hay cordgrass, 76
Maryland wild sensitive plant, 34, 35, 36
Matelea floridana, 45, 46, 47
Matelea pubiflora, 45, 46, 47
may haw, 42
meadow alexanders, 28
meadow joint vetch, 34
Megathymus cofaqui, 80
Megathymus yuccae, 80
Megisto viola, 60
Meske's skipper, 73
metamorphosis, 19
Michaux's croton, 51
Michaux's hawthorn, 42, 85
mistletoe family, 40
mock bishop's weed, 28
mockernut hickory, 39
Mohr's threeawn, 74
molt, 18
monarch, 18, 26, 45
monarch butterfly caterpillar, 26
monk skipper, 74
Morella caroliniensis, 41
Morella cerifera, 41
mound-lily yucca, 80
mudbank crowngrass, 58, 77, 79
mustard family, 32, 33
Myricaceae, 41
myrtle oak, 39, 41, 42, 65, 66, 67

N

narrow plumegrass, 69, 70, 72
Nastra lherminier, 77
Nathalis iole, 34
native nector sources – shrubs, 87, 88
native nector sources – trees, 85, 86
native nector sources – vines, 89, 90
native nector sources – wildflowers, 81, 82, 83, 84
needle palm, 74
Neonympha areolatus, 59
netted pawpaw, 31
nettle family, 53
northern bayberry, 41
northern cloudywing, 63
Nuttall's thistle, 51, 56
nymphs, 57

O

oak family, 39, 41, 42, 65, 66, 67
oak mistletoe, 40
obscure skipper, 75
ocola skipper, 75
Ocotea coriacea, 29, 30
Oligoria maculata, 78
orange barred sulphur, 35, 45
orange sulphur, 36
Orobanchaceae, 50
Orthosia scoparia, 45, 46, 47

P

painted lady, 51
palamedes swallowtail, 29
Palatka skipper, 75
palm family, 74, 76
palmetto skipper, 76
panicled ticktrefoil, 40, 61, 62, 63, 64
Panicum amarum, 68, 70, 75, 78
Panicum dichotomiflorum var. *Bartowense,* 68, 70, 71, 75, 78
Panicum hemitomom, 68, 70, 71, 75, 78
Panicum virgatum, 68, 70, 71, 75, 78
Panoquina ocola, 75
Panoquina panoquin, 76
Panoquina panoquinaoides, 75
Papilio cresphontes, 13, 28
Papilio glaucus, 30
Papilio palamedes, 29
Papilio polyxenes, 28

Papilio troilus, 30
Parietaria floridana, 53
Parietaria praetermissa, 53
Parrhasius m album, 42
parsley hawthorn, 42
partridge pea, 35
Paspalum bifidum, 58, 77, 79
Paspalum boscianum, 58, 77, 79
Paspalum botterii, 58, 77, 79
Paspalum caespitosum, 58, 77, 79
Paspalum conjugatum, 58, 77, 79
Paspalum dissectum, 58, 77, 79
Paspalum distichum, 58, 77, 79
Paspalum eglume, 58, 77, 79
Paspalum floridanum, 58, 77, 79
Paspalum leave, 58, 77, 79
Paspalum plicatulum, 58, 77, 79
Paspalum praecox, 58, 77, 79
Paspalum pubiflorum, 58, 77, 79
Paspalum repens, 58, 77, 79
Paspalum setaceum, 58, 77, 79
Paspalum vaginatum, 58, 77, 79
Passiflora incarnata, 48
Passiflora lutea, 48, 49
Passiflora suberosa, 8, 48, 49
Passifloraceae, 48, 49
passionvine family, 48, 49
pea family, 34, 35, 36, 38, 40, 62, 63, 64
pearl crescent, 37, 52
peninsula sedge, 58, 71
perennial glasswort, 39
perennial saltmarsh aster, 52
perplexed ticktrefoil, 40, 61, 62, 63, 64
Persea borbonia var. *borbonia,* 29, 30
Persea borbonia var. *humilis,* 29, 30
Persea palustris, 29, 30
phaon crescent, 18, 52
Phocides pigmalion, 62
Phoebis agarithe, 35
Phoebis philea, 35
Phoebis sennae, 20, 34, 44
Phoradendron leucarpum, 40
Phyciodes phaon, 52
Phyciodes tharos, 37, 52
Phyla nodiflora, 52, 55
piedmont blacksenna, 51
Pieris rapae, 32
pignut hickory, 39
pine barren fluff grass, 59

pinebarren ticktrefoil, 40, 61, 62, 63, 64
pineland butterfly pea, 38, 62
pineland false foxglove, 50
pineland waterwillow, 54
pinewoods bluestem, 72. 73, 78
pinewoods milkweed, 45, 46, 47
pineywoods dropseed, 75
pipevine swallowtail, 17, 29
pitch fork crown-grass, 58, 79
Pithecellobium unguis-cati, 35
Plantaginaceae, 55
plantain family, 55
Plukenet's false foxglove, 51
Plumbaginaceae, 38
plumbago family, 38
Plumbago zeylanica, 38
Poaceae, 58, 59, 60, 68, 69, 70, 72, 73, 75, 76, 77, 78, 79
Poanes aaroni, 68
Polites baracoa, 68
Polites themistocles, 78
Polites vibex, 12, 79
polydamas swallowtail, 29
Polygonia interrogationis, 52
pond apple, 31
pondspice, 29, 30
Pontia protodice, 32
poplar family, 54
Populus, 54
Populus alba, 55
Populus deltoides, 55
pretty false pawpaw, 31
prickly ash, 29
prickly bog sedge, 57, 71
primrose leaf violet, 49
privet wild sensitive plant, 34, 35, 36
Problema byssus, 69
prostrate blue violet, 49
Prunus americana, 54, 86
Prunus angustifolia, 54, 86
Prunus caroliniana, 54, 86
Prunus geniculata, 54
Prunus serotina, 24, 54, 86
Prunus umbellata, 54, 86
Ptelea trifoliate, 28
Ptilimnium capillaceum, 28
purple false foxglove, 51
purple passionflower, 48
purple thistle, 51, 56
purpletop fluff-grass, 59

Pursh's milkpea, 38, 40
Pyrgus communis, 65
Pyrgus oileus, 67
Pyrisitia lisa, 35

Q

Quadrella jamaicensis, 32, 33, 88
queen, 46
Quercus chapmanii, 39, 41, 42, 65, 66, 67
Quercus geminata, 39, 41, 42, 65, 66, 67
Quercus incana, 39, 41, 42, 65, 66, 67
Quercus inopina, 39, 41, 42, 65, 66, 67
Quercus laevis, 39, 41, 42, 65, 66, 67
Quercus laurifolia, 39, 41, 42, 65, 66, 67
Quercus margarettae, 39, 41, 42, 65, 66, 67
Quercus michauxii, 39, 41, 42, 65, 66, 67
Quercus minima, 39, 41, 42, 65, 66, 67
Quercus myrtifolia, 39, 41, 42, 65, 66, 67
Quercus nigra, 39, 41, 42, 65, 66, 67
Quercus pumila, 40, 41, 42, 65, 66, 67
Quercus virginiana, 40, 41, 42, 65, 66, 67
question mark, 52

R

rattlesnakemaster, 28
raven-foot sedge, 57, 71
red admiral, 53
red bay, 29, 30
red mangrove, 63
red spotted purple, 24, 53
red threeawn, 74
red-banded hairstreak, 41
reflexed sedge, 58, 72
Rhapidophyllum hystrix, 74
Rhizophora mangle, 63
Rhizophoraceae, 63
Rhus copallinum, 41, 86
rice button aster, 52
Rosaceae, 42, 53
rose family, 42, 53
rough dropseed, 75
roughfruit scaleseed, 28
running oak, 40, 41, 42, 65, 66, 67
rustyseed paspalum, 58, 77, 79
Rutaceae, 29

S

Sabal etonia, 74
Sabal minor, 74
Sabal palmetto, 74
Saccharum alopecuroides, 69, 70, 72
Saccharum baldwinii, 69, 70, 72
Saccharum giganteum, 69, 70, 72
sachem skipper, 76
Salicaceae, 54
Salicornia ambigua, 39
Salicornia bigelovii, 39
Salix caroliniana, 54, 55
Salix floridana, 54, 55
saltmarsh cordgrass, 76
saltmarsh false foxglove, 50
saltmarsh skipper, 76
sand cordgrass, 76
sand live oak, 39, 41, 42, 65, 66, 67
sand post oak, 39, 41, 42, 65, 66, 67
sandhill milkweed, 37
sandhill milkweed seed pod, 26
sandy woods sedge, 57, 71
Sanicula canadensis, 28
sassafras, 29, 30
Sassafras albidum, 29, 30
satyr butterflies, 57
Satyrium calanus, 39
Satyrium favonius, 41
Satyrium liparops, 41
Satyrodes appalachia, 57
savannah milkweed, 45, 46, 47
saw palmetto, 74, 75
scale-leaf aster, 52
scrub hickory, 39
scrub oak, 39, 41, 42, 43, 65, 66, 67
scrub palmetto, 74
scrub plum, 54
sea torchwood, 29
seashore dropseed, 75
seashore paspalum, 58, 77, 79
sedge family, 57, 71, 75
Seminole false foxglove, 50
Seminole Texan crescent, 54
Senna ligustrina, 34, 35, 36
Senna marilandica, 34, 35, 36
Senna obtusifolia, 34, 35, 36
Senna pendula var. *glabrata,* 44
sensitive pea, 35

Serenoa repens, 74, 76
Seymeria cassioides, 51
Seymeria pectinate, 51
shallow sedge, 58, 71
sharp-scale sedge, 58, 71
shiny wood-oats, 58, 59
shoreline sedge, 57, 71
short spike bluestem, 72, 74, 78
shyleaf, 34
sicklepod, 34, 35, 36
Sida ciliaris, 65, 67
Sida elliottii, 65, 67
Sida rhombifolia, 65, 67
Sida ulmifolia, 65, 67
sidebeak pencilflower, 34
silk bay, 29, 30
silver croton, 51
silver plumegrass, 69, 70, 72
silver-spotted skipper, 63
silvery cudweed, 50
Simmond's aster, 52
Simpson's crabgrass, 70, 73, 76
sleepy duskywing, 66
sleepy orange, 36
slender crabgrass, 70, 73, 76
slender Indian-grass, 59, 68
slender wood-oats, 58, 59
slender woodland sedge, 57, 71
slenderleaf false foxglove, 51
slimleaf pawpaw, 31
slimleaf ticktrefoil, 40, 61, 62, 63, 64
slimspike threeawn, 74
small fruit beggarticks, 35
smallflower pawpaw, 31
smooth beggarticks, 35
soft milkpea, 38, 40
soldier, 46
Sorghastrum elliottii, 59, 68
Sorghastrum nutans, 59, 68
Sorghastrum secundum, 59, 68
sour paspalum, 58, 77, 79
sourgrass, 70, 73, 76
southern broken-dash, 77
southern cloudywing, 63
southern crabgrass, 70, 73, 76
southern cutgrass, 73
southern dogface, 36
southern hairstreak, 41
southern magnolia, 30

southern pearly eye, 60
southern skipperling, 77
southern wild rice, 73
Spanish bayonet, 80
Spanish needles, 9, 35
sparkleberry, 42, 86
Spartina alterniflora, 76
Spartina bakeri, 76
Spartina cynosuroides, 76
Spartina patens, 76
Spartina spartinae, 76
Spermolepis divaricata, 28
Spermolepis echinata, 28
spicebush, 29, 30
spicebush swallowtail, 30
split-beard bluestem, 72, 74, 78, 79
spoonleaf cudweed, 50
Sporobolus compositus, 75
Sporobolus curtissii, 75
Sporobolus domingensis, 75
Sporobolus floridanus, 75
Sporobolus junceus, 75
Sporobolus virginicus, 75
spotted water hemlock, 28
spring cress, 32, 33
spurge family, 51
spurred butterfly pea, 38, 62, 89
St. Augustine grass, 60, 76, 77, 79
Staphylus hayhurstii, 62
Stenotaphrum secundatum, 60, 76, 77, 79
sticky joint vetch, 34
striped hairstreak, 42
Strymon melinus, 10, 40
Stylosanthes biflora, 34
Stylosanthes hamata, 34
sugarcane plumegrass, 69, 70, 72
sumac family, 41
summer farewell, 36, 82
swamp bay, 29, 30
swamp chestnut oak, 39, 41, 42, 65, 66, 67
swamp milkweed, 18, 45, 46, 47, 81
swamp thistle, 56
swarthy skipper, 77
sweet scented pigeon-wings, 62
sweetbay, 30
sweetgum tree, 15
switchcane, 60
switchgrass, 68, 70, 75, 78
Symphyotrichum adnatum, 52

Symphyotrichum bahamense, 52
Symphyotrichum carolinianum, 52
Symphyotrichum concolor, 52
Symphyotrichum dumosum, 52
Symphyotrichum elliottii, 52
Symphyotrichum lateriflorum, 52
Symphyotrichum pilosum, 52
Symphyotrichum simmondsii, 52
Symphyotrichum tenuifolium, 52
Symphyotrichum undulatum, 52
Symphyotrichum walteri, 52

T

tall ironweed, 50
tall threeawn, 74
tawny emperor, 15, 43
tawny-edged skipper, 78
tenlobe false foxglove, 51
Thalia geniculata, 69
thin paspalum, 58, 77, 79
Thorybes bathyllus, 63
Thorybes confuses, 61
Thorybes pylades, 63
threadleaf false foxglove, 51
Tiedemannia filiformis, 28
tiger swallowtail, 30
Tilia americana var. *caroliniana*, 53
Tracy's bluestem, 72, 74, 78, 79
trailing milkvine, 45, 46, 47
Trepocarpus aethusae, 28
Tridens ambiguous, 59
Tridens carolinianus, 59
Tridens flavus, 59
Trifolium carolinianum, 36
Trifolium reflexum, 36
Tripsacum dactyloides, 69
tropical checkered skipper, 67
tropical water hyssop, 55
tulip tree, 30
turkey oak, 39, 41, 42, 65, 66, 67
turkey tangle fogfruit, 52, 55
twin-spot skipper, 78
twoline false foxglove, 50

U

Ulmaceae, 53

Ulmus alata, 53
Ulmus americana, 53
Ulmus crassifolia, 53
Urbanus dorantes, 61
Urbanus proteus, 62
Urochloa adspersa, 58
Urochloa platyphylla, 58
Urtica chamaedryoides, 53
Urtica urens, 53
Urticaceae, 53

V

Vaccinium arboreum, 42, 86
Vanessa atalanta, 53
Vanessa cardui, 51
Vanessa virginiensis, 50
valamuerto, 44
variegated fritillary, 48
velvet-leaf milkweed, 45, 46, 47
velvetleaf ticktrefoil, 40, 61, 62, 63, 64
Vente conmigo, 51
Verbenaceae, 52, 55
Vernonia angustifolia, 50
Vernonia blodgettii, 50
Vernonia gigantea, 7, 50, 84
vervain family, 52, 55
viceroy, 54
Vigna luteola, 38
Viola bicolor, 48
Viola lanceolata, 48
Viola palmata, 48
Viola primulifolia, 48
Viola sororia, 48
Viola villosa, 48
Viola walteri, 49
Violaceae, 48
Viola's wood satyr, 60
violet family, 48
Virginia saltmarsh mallow, 40
Virginia snakeroot, 29, 30
Viscaceae, 40

W

Wallengrenia otho, 77
Walter's aster, 52
Walter's sedge, 58, 72

warty sedge, 58, 72
water cowbane, 28
water hickory, 39
water oak, 40, 41, 42, 65, 66, 67
water paspalum, 58, 77, 79
wavy leaf aster, 52
wax myrtle, 41
whirlabout skipper, 12, 79
white - m hairstreak, 42
white grass, 73
white nymph, 28
white oldfield aster, 52
white peacock, 15, 55
white poplar, 54
white tassels, 36
white twine-vine, 45, 46, 47
white-edge sedge, 57, 71
whorled milkweed, 45, 46, 47
Willdenow's sedge, 57, 71
willow family, 54, 55
winged elm, 53
winged sumac, 41, 86
wiregrass, 74
woolly croton, 51
woolly dutchman's pipe, 17, 29
woolly pawpaw, 31
woollysheath threeawn, 74

Y

yaupon blacksenna, 51
yellow Indian-grass, 59, 68
yellow passionflower, 48, 49
Yucca aloifolia, 80
Yucca filamentosa, 80
yucca giant skipper, 80
Yucca gloriosa, 80

Z

Zanthoxylum clava-herculis, 29, 86
Zanthoxylum fagara, 29
zarucco duskywing, 67
zebra longwing, 7, 8, 16, 23, 49
zebra swallowtail, 22, 31
Zerene cesonia, 36
Zizaniopsis miliacea, 73

Zizia aurea, 28
Zizia trifoliate, 28

www.ingramcontent.com/pod-product-compliance
Lightning Source LLC
Chambersburg PA
CBHW042336150426

43195CB00001B/7